The Secret
Wealth Building System
That Never Fails

GIVE TO GET

AMAZON BESTSELLING AUTHOR
JONATHAN GREEN

PRAISE FOR OTHER BOOKS
BY JONATHAN GREEN

SERVE NO MASTER

"If you are looking to escape your 9-5, *Serve No Master* is the book you need to read. Other people hype about leaving your 9-5 and how wonderful it will be. Jonathan Green tells you about his journey and gives you the tools to get started while keeping things in perspective. You will find no fluff or sugarcoating here. If you're looking for advice to get rich quick, move along.

Reading his writing is like sitting across from a trusted friend who is explaining to you how to break your chains and go after the life you want to live. It oozes with the authenticity of wanting you to succeed. Full of down-to-earth advice and encouragement to take action, this book is the perfect way to start your journey to serving no master.

I can't wait to start taking action and implementing all that I have learned."

– Carrie L.

○

"You truly have made my month! I really cannot explain how I came across your book on Amazon — it seemed like a dream. I read your reviews and saw that they were awesome, and I read your sample book and immediately bought it after. I just felt it was a good thing. After I bought your book, I signed up for a free trial of Audible and got your book and also signed up for a free trial of Kindle Unlimited to get your free book.

I have never listened to a podcast in my life! However, when I heard yours, I was hooked. There is something about you that silently screams genuine. I wish there was a way that we could hang out on the beach together as friends, because I feel that we would get along nicely.

Starting on my new journey towards financial freedom — I am a father of two, work full time, and in school full time. I love my life but definitely would like to have more cushion in my finances (Who wouldn't?). With so much info — Starting a blog! Affiliate marketing! Writing a book! — I must say I am overwhelmed and trying to find my direction. Nevertheless, your book spoke to me (literally, with a cool British accent)!"

If you are debating whether to buy this book because of the price, stop thinking about it. It is such a good book with information that will open you up to not just how to earn more income but also how to change your philosophy within your mind. A lot of what I struggle with when it comes to branching out, being brave, and working for myself, is that I do not have confidence."

I have read so many books on self-help and business, and this one, while it may not have been the most glamorous, it was real. I really felt that what I was reading came from a real person and would really help me."

– Josh B

o

"I had the chance to meet Jonathan Green, the author, and spend some time hanging out with him when we crossed paths during our travels in Asia. He told me about this book he had written, so I got my copy and read it in one night. I couldn't put it down, because it speaks so much truth — and I could relate to every word.

I also earn my money online (I've been running a successful online business for years), and I enjoy the same incredible freedom that Jon enjoys. Friends and family members of mine are constantly asking me to teach them what I do, because let's face it —

it is virtually impossible to get wealthy while living anywhere on the planet you choose to live if you continue to accept the same old mindset and work at a 9-5 job (where the purpose of our job is to make someone ELSE richer, while you are always expendable).

Consider yourself lucky that you live in the age of the internet. *Serve No Master* is a well-written, easy-to-follow playbook that explains how to harness the internet to quickly and effectively create an online business that can not only replace your job—it can potentially make you far wealthier than any job ever could.

And if you're thinking that you 'just don't have the time' or that you're too young, too old, or not in the right situation to capitalize on this information, this book contains very powerful motivational advice (and a lot of blunt truths) that are sure to light a fire under you.

My main takeaway from reading this fantastic book? You are the master of your own destiny. It's not about who wins the upcoming presidential election. It's not about depending on your boss or your company, or anyone else, to recognize your hard work. YOU are the only person on this planet who has the power to chart your course in life. And the internet has given all of us an amazing opportunity to build wealth and experience a life of freedom that never existed for any previous generation.

Serve No Master is one of the best books on this topic. Speaking as someone who 'broke the chains' of the corporate world and now lives every day however I want, wherever I want, in amazing and exotic countries — all thanks to my online business, which I started in my one-bedroom apartment years ago — I strongly encourage you to read this. It will open your eyes to endless new possibilities."

– Rob W.

○

THE POWER OF EXTREME GIVING

In this book, you will learn the power of Extreme Giving, a concept I began practicing long before writing this book. Here are a few comments from those who have been the recipients of my Extreme Giving:

"Your free books opened up a world for me that I would not have found without them. Thanks!"

– Astrid K.

○

"I also feel your positive, passionate energy as you intro the speakers and teach the topics in your course. I share with others about the courses you teach."

– Barry K.

○

"Jonathan Green's books, podcasts, and other materials have helped me keep my dreams alive and given me a very sound foundation in what I need to do to get there."

– Brandon B.

o

"That free book was so helpful; it led to me purchasing more of your books and courses, which have proven even more helpful."

– Charlie B.

o

"Jonathan, I loved your free book, *Fire Your Boss*. I have a 9-5, which I hated at the time I found your book. After reading all the ideas in this epic book, I started a copywriting and sales funnels sideline, which is growing rapidly, and I've now started enjoying my job as I know it's just a stepping stone to greater things."

– Claire B.

o

"Being generous is one way to say you are thankful for the generosity you have received. It is a privilege and a blessing. The cycle of generosity is a key element for a happy and fulfilled life. All I can say is both ways of generosity have helped me grow as a person, hence in the way I make a living.

Jonathan Green's generosity has impacted my life by opening my eyes to new horizons and possibilities. I really want to thank you, Jonathan. I have learned a lot from your books, audiobooks, blueprints, and courses. Your business model is inspiring, and so is your lifestyle. Thanks for your generosity in sharing and teaching everything you know and do."

– Jaime B.

○

"Jonathan is one of the few internet marketers and authors out there with true integrity. He always over-delivers, unsolicited; you don't have to be a customer to benefit from his wisdom, though if you do, you'll have no regrets."

– Jaye M.

○

"I've found that when you give generously with no expectation of something in return, you actually get more in return than you would have if you'd asked for something in the first place."

– Jeffrey T.

○

"Helping someone with no expectations has been invaluable in my business... definitely my 'secret' to unexpected successes!"

– John C.

○

"Jonathan Green, you are an amazingly generous human being. Thank you so much for all the free content you are always giving freely without any hidden agendas. Wishing you all the success in all your endeavors."

– Kevin S.

○

"I do like all the free stuff, but I have also bought products from you, and I do think the main reason I follow you and read your emails is because you always read mine and respond to them."

– Mary E.

○

"Your free giveaways are very helpful. They are of so much value that if they were for money, they could be difficult to afford. You're really one of those who contribute so much to make the world better. I am proud to state I am one of the disciples of *Serve No Master*."

— Norbert K.

o

"You are willing to share amazing content with no demands for those you share with."

— Patti P.

o

"This Jonathan Green character, he's one heck of a cool, super inspirational dude—he delivers value in spades and literally walks the talk on always giving generously to receive. Feast yourself on some sweet manna in his new book *Give to Get* and prepare for a life of overflowing abundance."

— Stephen T.

o

"Jonathan is amazingly generous with his information, help, encouragement, and advice. His web products have given me confidence in my own business; I know whenever I have a question, I can always find the answer on his website. His first book, *Serve No Master,* was an inspiration to me for getting involved in life on the web! He continues to serve as a model, mentor, and powerful example of what can be achieved."

– Tom L.

TABLE OF CONTENTS

FREE GIFT

I want to thank you for taking the time to grab a copy of *Give to Get*. I've spent ten years building a business on a foundation of Extreme Giving and I am so excited to transform your life. Over the coming pages, you will see exactly how to build an amazing business by focusing on giving, rather than selling.

This is the easiest and fastest way to grow a business, and it's allowed me to endure multiple market shocks.

This book is the foundation for an amazing business model... but it's just the beginning. In the second book, you will get step-by-step instructions on how to implement Extreme Giving. The book you hold in your hands is the big picture and the vision for creating an amazing business. When you're ready to take that business to the next level, you're going to LOVE *Give to Get Part 2: Advanced Tactics*. And it is yours. Absolutely free. When you click this link:

ServeNoMaster.com/Give

INTRODUCTION

For five days, not a single morsel of food passed through my lips. For five agonizing days, I put not a single calorie into my body. For five days, I had nothing to eat.

When you're starving, you learn who you are. Things that used to matter fade away, and you learn what true need is.

I was staring into the mirror for five days in a row, wondering how long I could last without telling anyone that I had no food and no money for food. I learned more about myself in those five days than in the rest of the forty years I've been around on this planet.

When all you're thinking about is survival, minor disagreements and conversations that used to seem so important fade into the ether. You don't care what TV shows are on, who has a crush on someone, or who's gossiping about what. None of that stuff matters. You find out who you are. You're forged through adversity and pain. And in that time of great testing, something happened that transformed who I am and how I approach business.

At the time, I was working for a charity. I traveled around the world from America to a small country called Wales, which is part of the United

Kingdom. I was part of an organization that helped inner-city kids find hope through music. As part of this program, I'd had to find financial support from back home.

I had about twenty people supporting me with anywhere from twenty to fifty dollars a month for a year. They'd agreed to fund me so I could do something good. Their support was wonderful, and it meant a lot. It allowed me to try to change the world, one person at a time.

One of the other people in the program hadn't raised enough support, so she was short every month. I agreed to give her a small part of my support as long as she would keep it a secret. To this day, nobody from our group knows that I was giving part of my support to her.

The first of those five days, I received fifty dollars from one of my supporters, and it was the day I was supposed to give her fifty to make ends meet.

I could have stretched that fifty bucks out, and that could have fed me for a week, but I had a decision to make. One of us was going to spend the next five days hungry, and I decided it was going to be me.

This was not a shared decision. I did not tell her it was my last fifty dollars; I just handed it to her. In that moment, with my back against the wall, I gave the last of what I had — the last of what I could give. I didn't just give her fifty dollars; I gave myself five days of suffering. When I came out on the other side, I was transformed and discovered a model for business and for life that opened the floodgates of opportunity and profit.

Over the following pages of this book, we are going on a journey together. I will reveal everything about the business model that has transformed my life from starving in a small village in Wales to living in a house bigger than I ever thought possible, on a tropical island where I go surfing nearly every single day.

We're going to go on a journey together that's going to forge you, transform you, and show you that if you can unlock the generosity within your heart, your business will never be the same. All the things you're worried about, all the fears you have, everything holding you back, will disappear. You will build a business that is recession-proof, trauma-proof, shock-proof, disaster-proof, and can endure and adapt to any environment.

Our ability to give is not finite.

To see the power of generosity in action, you can visit my website ServeNoMaster.com. I continually give away copies of training courses and books, and I can do that forever. The internet has opened a world of scalability for us where we can now give to more people than we could ever have met before. That's the greatest power that technology now affords us: to expand the power of our generosity.

Every single one of us has been through challenges and hard moments in life. Moments where we've been tested, moments where we wondered who we were, what we're made of. Are we cowards, or heroes? Are we brave? Are we survivors? On this journey, we're going to see that if you can put the giving first, everything else will follow.

In my business, I no longer need to chase profits. I don't look for more things to sell; I look for more things to give. I look for more people to reach, and my business is exploding because of this transformation.

CHAPTER ONE

The business we're going to build has three very simple components. These are all you need to build a business that will last the rest of your life and that you can pass on to your children. The three parts are traffic, engagement, and sales.

Extreme Giving is the core concept of this entire business model. The more content, value, and love you give to your audience, the faster your business will grow. It's the opposite mindset of many businesses, that treat visitors like garbage until they start spending money. The idea is to give more than your competition, and Extreme Giving is the central theme to a three-part business model:

- Traffic: Strangers are discovering you for the first time
- Engagement: You are building a relationship with visitors who enter your store
- Profit: Visitors are spending money and becoming customers

Every action I take falls into one of those categories. Sometimes, it may fall into multiple areas. That's a good thing! I love getting double benefits from the same action.

If I'm telling a story about my family and share an affiliate link at the end, that's both engagement and profit.

It's okay if you've never heard of me before reading this book. You might still be getting to know me, which means that we're in the traffic phase.

Every time I look at my business, I think about what I need to work on the most and where I need to put in the most effort. Right now, my profit area is very strong, but I need more traffic. To gain more traffic, I need to give away more free gifts and put myself in front of more audiences.

This year, I'm going to focus on traffic. Next year, I'm going to focus on a different area. But every year, I put a lot of effort into engagement. I began my business by building engagement, then I built profit, and now I'm building traffic. No matter my primary focus, I always remember my roots and keep my engagement strong.

You can rotate through the three components in different ways as you grow your business. Once you build an Extreme Giving business, you can pinpoint areas that need improvement and adjust your business accordingly.

Extreme Giving is not only the best way to grow your business when the economy is strong, but it is the answer to surviving a recession.

I'm writing this chapter in the throes of the COVID-19 pandemic, and I haven't been allowed to leave my house for two months. The worldwide economy is in turmoil, and I realized that more people need access to a business model that can keep working even when times are tough.

One of the most important lessons you can learn is to harness the power of scale. While it's more important to have active followers than a large email list, the larger your audience is, the more options you have to pivot and adjust your business.

If you have one hundred followers, there's only so much you can do to access those people. If you have one thousand followers, you have ten times as many options.

Extreme Giving allows us to adapt to economic downturns and pandemics through the power of scale.

Imagine that every person who follows you buys one of your products. If you have one hundred followers, and each one buys something for one hundred dollars, you make ten thousand dollars. If you have one thousand followers, you can drop that price down to ten dollars per person so that even when times are tough, your audience can still afford to buy your products, and you make the same amount of money.

This is one of the many ways in which the flexibility of this business model allows you to adapt. Even if you're selling physical products in larger units, as long as you achieve scale, you can lower your cost per unit and get into the world of unit economics.

Extreme Giving isn't just about information marketing; this is about all marketing and establishing relationships.

**Extreme Giving, in the simplest terms,
is giving more than people expect.
Give frequently, give often, and over-deliver.**

The idea that giving away too much will diminish your value is completely wrong. When we give something away for free, we demonstrate to people just how excellent our content is. If someone reads a free blog post and is impressed enough with the content, they will give you their email address in order to read one of your free e-books. If they enjoy that, they will assume that the content will be even better when they pay for it, and they will likely buy one of your paid books or courses.

Extreme Giving doesn't diminish your value—it increases it. When people like you, they will buy things from you.

TRAFFIC

The first component of any business is traffic, and it's where most new businesses fail. Traffic is how many people walk past the front door of your store. In the virtual world, it's how many people have heard your name. I spent a year working for that charity, and those five days of starvation were just one week out of fifty-two that I spent trying to transform young lives and show people that hope is possible. During that year, I had more traffic than my coworkers, because I was going to more events and spending more time being more available than everyone else in my program. I was where the kids were.

If you're not where your audience is spending time, then they will never find you.

One of the most common mistakes modern businesses make is to build a business that the owner wants rather than the business that the customers need. If you build your entire business on Facebook and your customers are on LinkedIn, they will never find you. Nothing else matters. Your prices, your engagement, and your product don't matter. If your audience only reads e-books and you're making paperbacks, they will never find you.

You must go where the people are, and you have to find where they spend their time. Before you build a business and before you open up a new revenue stream, you have to research.

Find out what your audience likes to do. What do your customers have in common with each other? Who is your ideal customer? What are their needs, their wants, their hopes, their dreams, their experience, their education? Do they have kids? Do they use social media? Which social media platform do they use when they're thinking about your industry?

If you're in the fitness space, your audience might use one social media platform to talk about fitness and another social media platform to talk about business, so you want to be sure you're in the right place to meet them when they're in the right mindset. To find where to meet your customers, you have to put in those extra hours and do extra research. You have to ask: where are these kids going?

Every Saturday morning during my time at that program, the friends I was working with would say, "Man, there was no one there last night. Where were all those kids?" But they never changed what they were doing. Empty, empty, empty.

If the customers aren't showing up, maybe you are in the wrong place.

Part of their failure was due to a lack of accountability. We weren't getting paid based on results; we weren't on commission. My coworkers would do the same thing, even though it wasn't working, over and over again. Why is no one here on Friday? They are somewhere. Teenagers will find something to do on a Friday, I promise you. I certainly did when I was in high school.

ENGAGEMENT

Engagement boils down to connecting with your audience. From the physical world to the digital, in its simplest form, engagement is having a conversation. If someone walks into your store and you have a friendly conversation with them, this is engagement.

Engagement occurs anywhere someone is enjoying your content. You can engage with followers while they're watching your videos, scrolling through your blog posts, or reading your book. You're engaging with me right now, because you're reading this book.

Whenever someone is paying attention to you, whether they're listening to you on a podcast episode or reading an email you've written, they're in the engagement phase. And that moment of connection is very important.

The engagement phase is where we're going to climb up the Ladder of Trust; you're going to give people what they expect and give people as much value as you possibly can at every point in the conversation. As people go from complete strangers, who have no reason to trust a word you say, to super fans who share your product with everyone, they climb the Ladder of Trust. At each stage in the relationship, you have to reconfirm their faith in you. This means you have to be at full energy each time you engage with a customer.

For a year and a half after my second son was born, my wife ran a hostel that we lived in. When she became pregnant with our fourth child, we decided to close it down. I asked my children if we should continue having guests or convert one of the dorms into an epic playground. The vote was unanimous.

Running the business and having so many children was wearing my wife down.

It turned out we made the right decision, because every hotel on our island closed down a few weeks later because of the pandemic.

Every single time a customer would come to stay with us, we had to be in a great mood and ready to repeat the same conversation with a smile on our faces. Who are you? Where are you from? What brings you here? How long are you staying? What are you passionate about? What are you looking to get from this experience?

These conversations are critical in any service business, especially tourism. If you don't give them enough friendliness, people will leave you bad reviews. We've had people say, "The other guests weren't friendly enough to me, so this hotel gets a bad review." Even when it's not your fault, a lack of engagement loses you those critical star ratings.

Nothing I'm saying to you in this book is original. Nothing I teach on my website is original. I am not the first person to teach that giving is good. I am not special. The only reason people follow me, read my emails, read my books, or buy from me is that they like me.

Getting people to like you across the digital divide can seem daunting, but I'll make it easy for you. People are all the same. We like authors, actors, musicians, and teachers that engage with us.

In every single one of my books, I say, "If you email me, I will reply." Every week I get emails from a new person who read one of my books and says, "Jonathan, I just emailed you to see if you'd actually reply."

Ta-da...surprise, I did! It feels fantastic when people who you think are unattainable reply to you. It makes you feel special. Five seconds of my day can make someone's week amazing. Why wouldn't I do that? The more value you give to people, the more likely they are to want to continue the relationship, and this can be in every single area of your life.

During my year of charity, I had more conversations with children who were in a place of low or no hope than all the other members of my organization combined. By the end of the year, the rest of the group hated me. They began to actively sabotage me.

They tried to get me kicked out of my apartment. They said horrible things about me, which weren't true. They really, really did not like me. At the end of the year, in our closing meeting, I said, "Guys, let me ask you a question. Do you remember, at the beginning of this year, when I said all I care about is the destination? I care about having a conversation with these kids and showing them that hope is a possibility. How many children that we worked with at the youth cafe and at the schools asked you about God, about changing their lives, or about their future?"

No one raised their hand.

I said, "Guys, the reason you don't like me is, every single one of you spent the last year failing. You're all great friends with each other. Congratulations. The people who gave you financial support to make a difference here, you stole from them because you didn't make a difference. Why? Because you have no engagement."

What difference does it make if customers are in your store if they never talk to you? Being in the same room with someone does not make them your friend.

One of my good friends asked me about a promotion I had last month. He thought the course I was recommending was amazing and a great fit for him. He listed three reasons why he wanted to make the purchase, but I still didn't think he should, because he just didn't have the money to buy it.

I tried to talk him out of it, but he bought it anyway, and he loves the program. He wanted the course, and he is still very dedicated to using it to help him build a very specific business model that got him excited.

While his situation worked out, I don't believe in going into debt to make money. I encourage you to go through my free courses and then pay for the more expensive courses from the profit you make when you implement those lessons.

Engagement is about more than fixing your audience's problems; it's about encouraging them to find the right path to success.

There are two key components of engagement. First, interact with your audience, give them advice, and help them with their problems. Second, interact with your audience in a way that will build trust.

While I'm happy that my friend likes the course he bought, the last thing I want to do is talk someone into buying a course that they will hate, because it could affect our friendship.

That's how I approach everyone in my life, and it's another way that you can engage with your audience to give more value than people expect.

When people message me and ask if they should buy something, they expect me to talk them into it. Most of the time, I try to talk them out of it, so I'm giving them more than they expected. Once the right opportunity presents itself, they will jump in with both feet. They will even want to buy through my link so I receive an affiliate commission, because I've earned their goodwill.

Engagement is very important. It is your free content, including videos, blog posts, or podcast episodes. It's all the content that you put out into the world to keep people's attention and gain their trust.

**Trust begins when people know that
the information you present is true.**

Some people write paid reviews. They write reviews because they've been paid a flat fee to do it, not because they use or like the product.

I see this on Instagram all the time. People pose with some dietary supplement that you know they've never used, because it never appeared in any of their pictures before they became beautiful. But now that they have a following that's big enough, suddenly this product that loves sponsorships appears next to them while they're wearing their tight, stylish exercise outfits.

Getting paid for your opinions is fine, but if people figure out that you're recommending something you don't use, or that you've said something that's not quite true, you're going to lose that audience, because you've broken their trust. People want you to say things you believe in.

The more levels of trust we have, the easier it is for people to make purchasing decisions. That's why engagement is so important.

This is a mistake that a lot of major brands make—they email you from the brand. Consumers don't buy from brands; we buy from people. That's why they need celebrities and other spokespeople to become the face of the brand.

So many companies have worked so hard to run ads for a brand, but no one buys from companies anymore. They buy from people, because they want to be like the person they admire and trust.

Engaging with your audience will help you build something powerful and successful, and building trust will ensure that you keep your audience close to you for years to come.

THE SALE

The third component of any successful business is the sale, where the profit happens.

Profit is the money you earn from things such as writing reviews, giving recommendations, sending people to your toolbox page, selling products, or sharing affiliate links. It can even come from sponsorships and Patreon supporters.

During my year of charity, I made the sale because I was continually engaging with the kids. With every business, the goal is to get to the sale. The sale during this year was to have "the conversation." The one every charity worker dreams of. The one where the teenager opens up and reveals their deepest fears, and you have that amazing hug at the end. The one where making a difference might just actually happen.

That was the goal of every conversation: to have enough of a relationship that the kids would ask me those questions. They would want to know more. They would want to know that there was something more available for them, and they were allowed to have hope.

If you don't have traffic, and you don't have engagement, then the sale will never happen. In my current business, the sale is selling products and generating revenue—making money. If you don't connect with your audience, answer emails, answer social media, and post content all the time, then people will forget you. They will move on to something else. They will get distracted.

If you don't put out new episodes of your television show all the time, people will start watching something else. Each new season, you try to recover all those people who started watching something else while you were on vacation.

The sales are the least important part of the Extreme Giving process, because they will always come. As long as you know from the beginning what you want to sell, you can structure your business in such a way that people have a natural moment at the end of the journey where buying makes sense, and then the sales will fall into place. If you start a blog about fishing and then you want to sell yoga equipment, it won't make sense.

You must create a logical progression from the beginning to the end of the relationship, where people can buy what you're selling — even if the sale is when your customers ask you questions like, "Am I better than my parents tell me I am? Am I more than my teachers say I'm capable of? Am I valuable?"

If you go where your customers are, have meaningful conversations, and speak to them with respect, they will buy from you. Because they like you, they trust you, and they feel a connection with you, the sales will fall into place. Traffic, engagement, and sales are the only three components of an Extreme

Giving business. When you bring those three components together, your business will go the distance.

In the end-of-the-year meeting with my coworkers, I ended the conversation by talking about sales.

"Do you know how many kids asked me about how I can party without enhancements? About how I feel about God and religion? About how I feel about parents? Do they have hope? Can they be something more than what they've been told? Can they be something bigger? Guess what? While you guys have hated me, nearly every single kid that I met this year, at some point, asked me. Not once did I bring it up.

"I never walked up to a kid and said, 'Hey, let me talk about your parents. Let me talk to you about God.' I don't do that. My goal this year was to transform this city. Guess what? None of these kids will remember you guys next year. A new group of people will come in here, and who knows what will happen—but I had those conversations."

By focusing on Extreme Giving and engagement, the sales just happened. I'm not a hero. I'm just a regular person who spent as much time near my customers as possible, gave more than everyone else in my market, and treated them the way they wanted to be treated. In the end, they asked for the sale.

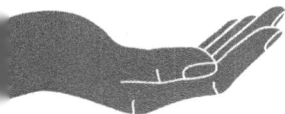

CHAPTER TWO

I want to transform your life, and I'm going to make it easy for you. I want to teach you the most important concept in this book right now - rather than making you read all the way to the end to get to the big nugget of secret. If you want to transform your life and transform your business, you need to embrace Extreme Giving.

The more that you give to your audience, the faster your business will grow.

In the very first meeting during my year and a half journey in the country of Wales, my team had a conversation. Everyone was asked, "What's more important, the journey or the destination?" There were about ten of us in the group, and everyone else said, "The journey. I want to form friendships. I want to form connections. I want this to be the best year of my life."

As usual, I was the outlier. I said to this group of people with their bright eyes and bushy tails, "Guys, I'm not here for you. My supporters are paying me to help people who have no hope to see that there is hope. They are not paying me to form relationships or friendships with you. I have one goal, and that is to have conversations with teenagers about hope. Some of those conversations will be about religion. Most of them will simply be about self-worth, helping them to believe that they are capable of accomplishing something, and encouraging them to believe in themselves."

The rest of the group looked at me like I was a monster. Their belief system was very different from mine. My goal, more than anything else, was to give people hope that they had been missing. I made some mistakes in my teenage and college years, and I hoped that I could undo some of my karmic damage by putting more goodness into the world. I realize that I am mixing metaphors and mixing religions; I apologize for that.

I believe that the world would be a better place if every one of us tried our best to put more good into the world than we take out of it. You can boil down my belief system into that core idea. I'm not sure that there's an arbiter of karma sitting out there measuring what everyone is due, but I believe in doing more good than I do bad.

Because I had done a lot of things that I regretted, I came to Wales with a single goal: have a transformative year. I said, "I want to give people more than they've ever received before." That's the core of Extreme Giving.

Extreme Giving is not just something I teach; this is what I live. If you join a market that I'm in, you're one more person with whom I can cooperate. You're not my competition. You're my potential partner. You're an opportunity, and that is why this is such a beautiful business model.

This book is not going to flood the market with competition; It's going to flood the market with new allies.

Extreme Giving is not about keeping secrets or worrying about losing your market share. None of that will happen, because we're all working together to give people a better experience and create amazing things.

I have a medical condition with my vision that affects everything I do. When I use the computer too much, my eyes hurt. Sometimes, "too much" can be as little as five minutes. When my eyes start to hurt, I have a range of symptoms, from itchiness to unstoppable crying, from a mild headache to temporary blindness. Sometimes, these symptoms can last for up to six weeks.

I do everything I can to use my computer as little as possible. When I communicate with my team and my employees, I send them voice messages from my phone. When I have to use a computer, I use e-ink reader tablets to avoid hurting my eyes.

When my vision went bad for the first time, I decided to build a business that could continue to work and generate revenue, even if I went completely blind.

The thought of going blind haunts me. If you've had a similar scare, you know the kind of fear I'm talking about. Every single day, I wonder if today is going to be the day that it happens. It's the ghost that haunts every single conversation that I have. I am always thinking about it. Whenever I have a few good weeks, I start to convince myself that I am cured. And then my old nemesis comes back, my eyes start hurting, and my vision starts fading.

That is one of the hardest paragraphs I've ever written. If you meet me in person, I'll have a smile on my face and I'll chat about growing your business. But in the back of my mind, that fear still hovers. It's always with me, threatening to take away my business and destroy my ability to support my family.

Extreme Giving is my answer to that fear. It's a business model that can survive every market shock the industry throws at me. It doesn't matter if Amazon bans my account, if my books are kicked out of the Google Play Store, or if my favorite program to recommend goes out of business. With the Extreme Giving model, I can adapt and pivot... even if my world goes dark.

I'll never forget when I was fighting in a judo match in Japan against a student who was much younger and smaller than me. While I was trying to choke him out, he was pulling me over his back, moving as slow as a turtle. I had size, strength, and mass on my side, but he had technique, and that was the force of inevitability.

It took him twenty minutes, but he eventually threw me over his shoulder and smashed me to the floor. At first, I was so annoyed that I hadn't been able to use my strength and power against him. Writhing on the ground, I had a moment of painful clarity; I realized that superior technique will always defeat brute force, even in business.

That is what Extreme Giving is. It's a business model that adapts and grows stronger when it's attacked.

That journey is what I'm going to share with you throughout this book. I'm going to teach you everything you need to know to build a powerful business, and we're going to start by talking about how to make some real money.

GIVE 'TIL IT HURTS

If you join my mailing list, follow me on social media, watch my videos on YouTube, or engage with me through any digital medium, you'll see that I take part in giveaways all the time. No matter what type of business structure you're using, there is something that you can give to your community and to your potential customers that will forge a powerful relationship.

Robert Cialdini talks about the Law of Reciprocity in his book *Influence.* The law of reciprocity says that if someone gives you something, you'll want to give them something back, even if it's something small.

Now you know why they give you free cookies when you walk into an open house. They are hoping that those free cookies will make you just a little bit more likely to make an offer on that house. That's why car salespeople keep coins in their pockets. Have you ever noticed how they make a big production of pulling coins out of their pocket to buy you a drink that costs two or three dollars? They want you to notice those loud coins clinking into the machine. It would be far cheaper for them to stock a staff refrigerator, but they know that you're more likely to buy a car from the person who just bought you a drink. You'll say to yourself, "He just bought me a drink; I've got to give him something in return."

This principle of reciprocity gets more powerful the more you give from a place of true giving. You can try to use reciprocity manipulatively. You can give people gifts with the sole intention of getting them to buy something from you later, but it will be of limited value. Extreme Giving works far better when it comes from a place of true giving.

I enter giving competitions all the time. Whether I am taking part in a book giveaway, a conference, a product bundle, or going to a birthday party, I always want to give the best gift. Often the other givers aren't even aware that there is a competition. The best gift doesn't have to be the most expensive, but it should be the one that the receiver likes the most.

I spent a year working in a youth cafe and volunteering at events with the other members of the charity. I only started to make a real difference when I went beyond expectations. While everyone else would go to the pub at the end of their workday, some kids still had to go home to families that didn't treat them right. Some of them had to go home and be hungry. Some of them had to go home and be afraid.

I still don't know how to work a part-time job. I don't know how to stop thinking about work when the steam whistle blows. Despite my best efforts, I've turned into my father, who went into work every Saturday that I can remember. I always said I would never become a workaholic, and yet my greatest struggle now is to limit how much I work.

I had a conversation with my father recently where he said, "Make sure you don't work more than six and a half days a week." That was the conversation he had with me. I was like, "Right, take off a half-day a week." It's hard for me to do even that much. I can't think of the last time I went an entire twenty-four hours without doing any work. It's not in my DNA.

The other volunteers would say, "The cafe closes at eight, so we don't have to do anything after that." Many of the kids would walk out of the cafe, go across the street and hang out in a public park, because they had nothing else to do. Guess what?

Kids at night in public parks... we all know that doesn't lead to good things! Unlike my coworkers, my shift end when the clock struck eight. I would hang out with the kids later, hang out with the kids earlier, and go further.

This is not a story about how I'm a great person. This is a story about me trying to be a better person, trying to transform myself, and trying to make a difference. Some people have no hope, and that's the worst thing that can happen to anyone, especially a child.

FREE DOESN'T MEAN CHEAP

I've traveled around the world, worked with many amazing people, and made friends with people from both ends of the financial spectrum. When I went to nightclubs, I would run into one of my friends who was a multi-millionaire, and he would give away champagne that I could never have afforded.

As he handed me a glass of champagne, I realized that if I continued to hang around him, I would get free stuff. The important detail is that *the free stuff was good*, which is where a lot of businesses drop the ball.

If you visit my website and go through my content, you'll see that I've put a lot of effort into giving you amazing stuff for free. I give away over a dozen different guides on building an email list, blogging, learning to be an affiliate marketer, or making your first dollar online. Whatever you're interested in, my team and I will constantly pour value into your need.

While my free guides aren't as long as books like this one, they take months to complete, because I put so much effort into their graphics and design. I want you to look at each of my guides and feel you are holding something valuable and beautiful in your hands.

The design of the guides isn't meant to cover up inferior content; it's there to enhance the content, which works. If you read the guides and implement what you learn, you should make money. I want you to be successful, and I do everything I can to help you reach your goals.

If you visit a website, download a beautiful guide, implement its process, and then make money, would you come back to that website for more information? Would you be willing to pay for one of the more expensive training courses to make even more money?

Of course you're going to come back. I would, too!

Whenever someone visits my website to buy something that they can't afford, I tell them to go through my free training and make money first. I would much rather you make money from my free content, than go into debt buying my paid courses. Not only will you have total faith that my content works, but you'll also be spending from profits, which is another principle that's very important to me.

I want to give you content that works; it's not just about perceived value.

The more you give, the stronger your relationship with your audience will be. This is the Entourage Effect: If someone receives free stuff every time they hang out with you, they're going to stick around, even if they don't like you. There is a reason that celebrities have such large entourages. Even the bottom member of the entourage gets free stuff.

And when the members of your entourage actually like you (because of your engagement), your relationship becomes bulletproof.

You can use this effect to create fanatics and followers who are addicted to you. Give them value and demonstrate that you care about them. This is the core of Extreme Giving.

Give people valuable content and exceed their expectations to establish a powerful relationship.

This is a critical rung in the Ladder of Trust, which I'll cover in more detail when we talk about engagement.

Each time you give something to your audience, you must meet or exceed their expectations, or they will stop trusting you.

Extreme Giving matters at every level of your business, and it goes beyond just free stuff. Every product you sell should be worth ten times the price in value. If someone buys a product for seven dollars, it should be worth seventy. They should always get massive value for a tenth of the cost.

People should know that every dollar they spend with you will earn them ten dollars in value. When they receive this much value, they're likely to buy more expensive products because they know that they're getting a massive return on their investment.

I'm not just teaching you how to build a following. I'm also teaching you how to become a great product creator and build a powerful business that helps people.

A core philosophy of Extreme Giving is intent. In the next few chapters, we're going to talk about Extreme Giving in terms of purpose. You can give lots of value, but it shouldn't be random. We want to give value to your customers, clients, and employees so that they stick with you for a very long time. That is the purpose of Extreme Giving.

The Extreme Giving principle is impossible to fake, because you must give massive amounts of value for it to work. When you do, your business will thrive, and you'll be unstoppable.

'TIL THE BREAK OF DAWN

The musical culture in the United Kingdom differs from the musical culture in America. When I went to high school in America, everyone wanted to play the guitar, while everyone in the UK wanted to learn to DJ. Turntables are expensive. I brought mine with me from America to the UK, and I allowed kids to use it all the time. We brought turntables to school events, so children could discover they had musical abilities.

I remember one child I worked with. Both of his parents lived off money from the government and had never worked a day in their lives. They told him he would end up just like them, living off the government when he graduated. They had no aspirations for themselves, and they had no aspirations for him.

He was one of the kids who spent a lot of time at our after-school cafe, so I spent a lot of time talking to him. He was also one of the more popular kids with the other volunteers. They really thought they were making a difference, because they were available Monday through Friday for a few hours after school. Once a month, they might see him at one of our weekend events.

Unlike my coworkers, who clocked out the moment they were allowed to, I hung out with him dozens of times outside of "office hours."

In between the school events, like most teenagers, he would go to any concert that would let him through the door. This is where I continued the connection. He saw me outside of the work environment where my coworkers spent all their time.

I love music events. I've traveled around the world and seen all the DJs and live bands that I liked. I've been to raves and festivals all over the globe. I'm passionate about dance music, and I make it happen - whether I am sleeping in a tent, in a bathtub, on the floor, or in the corner of a crack den (which I have done—big mistake). Whatever it takes to see that next musician.

When you go to these types of events, sometimes you need a bit of an accelerator or a mood enhancer to help you stay up all night. We've all experimented in our own ways, and while in college, I reached a moment of transformation when I realized I couldn't do this anymore, or I'd die.

By the time I arrived on the shores of the United Kingdom, I was transformed. Without enhancement, I would go to rave after rave. Some of these events were in the most amazing locations, ranging from the beach to the woods and many places in between — and once, I even went to a rave in a castle.

At most of these events, the main DJ doesn't even take the stage until 2 am. And the party often goes on long past the rising of the sun.

BETTER LIVING THROUGH CHEMISTRY

More than a few times, someone has asked, "Hey, Jonathan, how do you last all night? How can you have fun? How can you enjoy these parties with no enhancers?" And I would say, "I just love the music. I love it so much, and I love having such a good time."

My goal and my job were to show people it's possible to have a fantastic time without needing to do things that will slowly eat away a piece of your soul. You still do the same thing as everyone else: stay up all night, see all the best DJs, party like a maniac. At a lot of these raves and festivals, I would see those fourteen- and fifteen-year-old kids from the youth cafe. Sometimes they were enhanced, and sometimes they weren't. For me, it was the consistency, the willingness to give that extra time, and realizing that I'm never off the clock, because they're always watching. That's what it means to give and to be an Extreme Giver.

In my current business, I always have the same conversation when I take part in giving events. It's the same whether I'm giving a talk, a book, or one of my courses.

I had this conversation with someone on Friday. The organizer said, "We're going to have twelve people give away twelve bonuses as part of this program." I asked, "Who's giving away the best thing?

What is it worth? Sixty-seven dollars? Okay, I'm going to give away something for ninety-seven."

I have to give the best - every single time.

If you join my mailing list, I send you a gift on day one. When you first meet me, I say, "Hey, if you join me and you become a follower, I'll give you a book or a PDF or training or invite you to join one of my groups." Day two, I say, "Surprise, here's another gift." Day three, I go, "Double surprise, here's gift number three." And if I find out one of you reads these books and starts giving away three gifts like I do, then I'm going to have to give away four.

I refuse to be the second-best giver.

I was recently told that I'm not allowed to participate in some of the giving events I've done in the past, because I make the other participants look bad. The person who organized these events said, "Look, you can't give away like this. We know that you're making a lot of money from building a massive audience because people take your product, and they don't look at anyone else's."

My response was, "You know what? If your mindset is to tell the person who's giving too much value and love to your customers to cut it out, you have a problem with your business model. I have no problem finding other ways to give away amazingness."

PRISON BREAK

There are far too many people who think they will never be free. They have given up. You could be one of them. There are people who think they'll never be able to escape the job they hate or the boss who despises them.

There are people who think they'll spend the rest of their life begging for a raise of a nickel or a dollar an hour. They're wondering if they'll ever pay off their credit cards, their mortgage, or their student loans. That kind of weight on your shoulders is crippling.

I can't give you a business. I can't put it in your hands, because you won't know how to run it and you won't know what to do with it. I can't kidnap you from prison and put you on the streets. What I can do is give you a blueprint, an escape plan, and the tools and training you need to implement them.

For every single person who visits my website, I have a training course where I walk you step by step through how you can make a thousand dollars this month. If money is tight, don't buy anything from me. Go through this training and make that extra grand. Then you can afford any of my courses.

Extreme Giving is about me giving, not what you do with the gift. I have no control over that. I can show you the blueprint to freedom, but I can't force you to use it.

Many years ago, my parents gave my oldest sister their old car as a high school graduation present. She sold it. They couldn't be mad at her for not using the gift in the way they'd intended. That would mean it wasn't a gift, but rather, an obligation. They had to let her decide how to use the gift.

It's still a funny story, because it definitely caught my parents by surprise, but they had to accept it. Once they gave my sister the car, it was no longer theirs. Since then, the tides have changed, and one of my other sisters recently gave my mom her old car. Sometimes the cycle of life reverses.

My mom still drives the car; she didn't turn around and sell it immediately. I don't know if you can do that to your kids, but again, when you give something, it has to be without strings.

All I can do is put hope, an escape plan, and value in front of every single person I encounter. I can do everything I can to support them and hope that they take the action that will transform them. In the same way, I hope you finish reading this book, because this will transform your life.

I can't tell you how many Monday mornings I had to listen to my coworkers complaining about their empty weekend events. I knew exactly where all those missing kids were. They were with me at a rave in a castle. I went to where the kids were.

That little extra mile of availability made all the difference.

The power of Extreme Giving is that the more you focus on giving, the more the sales role in. When you focus on giving, you will always get the profit you need.

CHAPTER THREE

I got into a brutal bathroom fight in eighth grade. When the fight started, there were a couple of other kids watching. By the time I walked out of the bathroom, there were more than fifty kids crowding the hallway, waiting to congratulate the victor.

It was not me.

Even a flawed business will make a lot of money if it gets the attention of a large crowd. Many businesses sell out of their inventory after an appearance on a popular television show. They weren't ready to handle so many customers, and they end up months behind. Sometimes they even have to cancel orders.

Even if the rest of your business isn't in place, when you put enough people in your store, you'll have massive success. You'll have success so big that your website can't handle it.

If you take a business living off of hundreds of visitors a day and put a million visitors through the front doors, that company is going to explode.

That's how powerful traffic is. Without traffic, nothing else happens. If no one walks through the front door, you have zero business, no matter how nice your store is.

GO WHERE THE PEOPLE ARE

EXTREME BLOGGING

Let's take a moment to get practical. It doesn't help very much if I tell you to go find your audience without telling you how to do it. One of the first places we can start is with the wonderful world of blogging.

Look for blogs in your niche that already have a lot of traffic. Then, look at which posts have the most comments and views. Your audience will read and comment on posts that interest them. They will tell you with their actions which topics they care about.

If you go to a diabetes blog, you might be surprised by which posts have the most comments. Maybe it's a post about how to give yourself your first shot, how to give a shot to someone you love, or how to help someone you love deal with their diabetes.

From this research, you will realize that people who read these blogs are not just people with diabetes, but also the loved ones, spouses, and children of people with diabetes.

While I haven't done a deep dive into diabetes blogs, I know that it's a possibility that the most popular blog article might be aimed toward someone who doesn't have diabetes at all.

In many of the medical niches that I've studied in the past, spouses spend more money than the person who actually has the disease, because they want to save their loved ones. I certainly put a lot more effort into my wife's medical care than I do my own. Articles catering for loved ones are often the most popular posts on medical blogs.

In addition to seeing which posts are most popular, you can also look at what the blog gives away. Look at the content they are using to generate sales, the products they are promoting, the types of product reviews they post, and how they monetize their website. They know what their audience is interested in, and you shouldn't let all their market knowledge go to waste.

Once you've combed through a blog to find out exactly who the audience is and what they're interested in, you can use that information to find and connect with them.

DISCUSSION GROUPS

Discussion groups can have various names and platforms. Whether it's a chatroom, forum, or Facebook group, a discussion group is any place where people gather to talk about interests. Even if you're building a business with a physical location, you can find relevant online communities built around your city.

The difference between a forum and a blog is that a forum completely centers around conversation, and the person who writes the first post will often reply to the comments.

Discussion groups have massive amounts of value, and you can often sort the threads by popularity. Most platforms will even tell you how many views and replies each post has. Looking at the most popular forum posts and comments will tell us what people are interested in talking about, from their biggest pain points, problems, and struggles to their desires, hopes, and ambitions.

All of this is useful information for your Extreme Giving business.

A forum is also a place where you can find people who will find value in what you have to offer to their audience. When you come from a place of giving value rather than taking, it's much easier to form alliances with these platforms and grow your business.

Many of these forums are run by people who love their audience and care for them a great deal, but they have no idea how to monetize their following properly or just haven't crossed that bridge. They have a huge audience, but they don't do much with it, and therein lies your opportunity.

Whether you're adding your content by writing high-quality posts, engaging with the moderators and audience, or even just paying for advertising to give away your free gift, coming from a place of beneficence allows you to really engage with that potential audience.

SOCIAL MEDIA

People communicate in very different ways on each social media channel, which is why so many social media channels exist. Different audiences require different platforms.

Choose the platform that your audience uses the most.

If you're a fitness person, it makes a lot more sense to seek out your audience on Instagram than on Twitter. Instagram is a more visual medium, which allows you to show off your muscles or beautiful abs.

If you're targeting C-level executives, business owners, or people who are focused on business growth, then LinkedIn is probably going to be the social media platform you want to approach.

People also spend different amounts of time on different channels. A teenager might spend much more time scrolling through Facebook than a business executive, who is just checking their LinkedIn messages.

The age of your audience, the problems they have, and their preferred mode of communication will be different for each social media channel, and you want to find the channel where your particular audience spends the most time.

Join the groups, follow the pages, and learn the hashtags that your group uses, so that you can jump into the conversation. You should join the conversation with the goal of giving value by offering help or sharing your experience.

Our goal is to approach our potential audience in a way that they find engaging and intriguing rather than annoying and offensive. We also want to remember the key aspect of the Extreme Giving model: give!

If you're constantly giving, it becomes easy to advertise your products later on.

If you jump into a conversation and immediately ask someone to buy your product because it sounds like they have a problem, people are going to push back. But if you join the conversation from a place of integrity and demonstrate your desire to actually help your audience and provide them with valuable information for free, they will happily listen to what you have to say, because you've built up that value first.

PODCASTS

I love podcasts because you can capture your audience's undivided attention. When someone is listening to a podcast, they aren't listening to anything else. There are platforms where you can be interviewed, give talks, hold giveaways, or be a sponsor.

It's important to know which podcasts your audience listens to and the content that interests them.

I always start by digging into the iTunes catalog. This is a great jumping-off point, since iTunes invented podcasts. Then you can look through other podcast catalogs. Be proactive and look for lists of the top podcasts in your genre, then look at all the guests who have appeared on those shows. Many of these guests will have smaller podcasts that are much easier to book an appearance on.

The beauty of podcast advertising is that if you put an ad on an episode of someone's podcast, your ad is there forever, whether someone downloads that episode today - or in ten years. New listeners are always hearing your message for the first time. This is a really powerful and effective strategy for getting your message out there and finding new followers.

The more strategic you are when looking for people who can hear your voice, the better. When you pay attention and try to understand your potential audience, it will be easier to connect with them and turn them into your audience.

BREAK THE BOX

There are always new platforms coming out and rising to prominence.

If you want to enter the streaming world, find the streamers who are most like you, and see which of their videos get the most traction. Look for the top posters on Reddit or Quora to find people you can work with and learn from. If your audience's favorite social media platform is Vine (which no longer exists), then look for ways to partner with great "Vine stars."

The platform doesn't matter nearly as much as our strategy. Find where your new audience spends time and then find the people they listen to. Find a way to offer people value, which we'll cover in the chapter on Extreme Alliances, and you are off to the races.

While the Extreme Giving system was created with online businesses in mind, it can work for any business with a few tweaks.

If you own a local brick-and-mortar business, you can still find your potential customer pool online simply by adding your location to your searches. It might be more important to focus on a pool of people who are close to your business for your data.

You can also gather data from your competitors, even if you are not an online-based business. If you want to know what's selling best in your competitor's shop, just look at the items displayed with the most prominence. Items in the bargain bins are the ones you definitely want to stay away from, because they're obviously not selling as well as something displayed proudly in the window.

While your competitors might not be online-based, you can still look at their online presence to gather information for your own business. Read all of the online reviews for these businesses. If you can understand the cause of the negative reviews, you can make sure that visitors to your business don't repeat that experience.

Whatever platform your audience uses to engage with the world, take the time to listen to what they are saying. People leave comments because they want you to read them, and it's the easiest way to give your audience exactly what they want.

The data is out there; we just have to get creative in finding it for your particular market.

COMPETITIVE INTELLIGENCE

Thirty years ago, companies paid millions of dollars to find out what their audience wanted. Today, we have the tools at our disposal to find out what our audience wants for free; we just have to pay attention.

Learning from social media is free. All you have to do is find your competition, join their mailing list, follow their Facebook page, or watch their YouTube channel. You can learn how they communicate with their followers, which of their posts get the most comments and replies, and which of their YouTube videos have the most and least views.

All of this information tells you what you should speak to your audience about, what type of messaging you should use, where your audience is spending the most time, and what interests them the most.

We don't have to guess which formats do well for each topic, because we can look at what everyone else is doing. We can easily find the places where our target audience is already hanging out, and we don't have to spend millions to find them.

With just a few hours of targeted research, you should have a list of blogs, discussion groups, social media channels, and podcasts that your audience enjoys. And the best part is that each of these lines of communication is owned by someone that you can collaborate with.

In a single afternoon, you can develop a real feel for who your audience is, what they respond to, and where you can find them.

So many people post amazing books, free gifts, or courses on their websites, but they have no idea who they're trying to find or where those people are spending their time. They end up shotgunning their approach and spend ten minutes a day on several different social media channels, when they could get better results if they just spent an hour a day on the one that matters.

Finding out where your audience doesn't spend time is just as important as finding out where they do spend time. If you've been in business for a while, you might discover that you've invested a lot of time in a channel that your audience doesn't care about.

If your niche is for people with diabetes, it won't benefit your business to spend all of your time on a medical health blog where no one has diabetes. You're almost in the right area, but you've missed the boat, because everyone with diabetes is on the diabetes-specific medical forum.

This is a lesson that's easier to learn now than waiting until your niche has dried up completely.

We want to see where people are spending time, what they're talking about, what interests them, and what words and language they use. All of this will help you communicate with your audience as you begin marketing and growing your relationship with your followers.

There are always people ready to receive Extreme Gifts; we just have to find them.

SHOW THAT YOU BELONG

Whilst I was living in Wales, there were many, many amazing DJs I wanted to see, and I wanted to have some British experiences that I couldn't access in my town at the edge of nowhere. You can travel to just about anywhere in Britain on a train ride of a few hours. It's amazing and magical.

I took trains to the Godskitchen nightclub in Birmingham, the Heaven club in London, and many other nightclubs that I'd heard about, but never seen. If I was going to take a night off from working with these amazing kids, I wanted to do something truly memorable. And seeing awesome DJs also gave me something to talk to those kids about when I got back.

I got to see some of the best DJs in the world, meet amazing people, and do things I never thought possible for a guy like me. And, along this journey, some amazing things happened. The very first time I went to London, I said to myself, "One of these nights I'm going to go to some of these events."

I had a flyer for an event I wanted to go to, but I realized that I didn't dress like these kids. I went to this little shop in North London called Cyberdog. I walked up to a sales assistant dressed like a detective from The Matrix and said, "I want to go to this party. Help me create a costume that will make me fit in."

I quickly discovered that people don't appreciate it when you call their clothes a costume. Despite using the wrong word to ask for help, I walked out of there with an amazing outfit.

Because I looked like I belonged, I started forming amazing friendships.

One night, I was wearing my new clothes in Godskitchen in Birmingham. I had ridden a four-hour train to a city I'd only read about online, found the nightclub in the dark using the rudimentary map on my phone and went inside to see two of my favorite DJs play for six hours straight.

Well past midnight, I'm standing in a nightclub in a foreign city in a foreign country, and I don't know a single person. I have clothes to fit in—certainly not a costume, never call it a costume—but I don't know anyone there. The music is amazing, as two fabulous DJs take turns playing records to see who can get the crowd going the craziest.

The lasers are flashing; the music is pumping, and I'm wandering around all alone. And then it happens.

I commit the original sin.

I bump into a gorilla—if gorillas were hairless with one percent body fat. This guy was massive. When he turned around, I thought, "Oh no." I don't even know what happens when you get beat up in England. I started to wonder about international insurance and reconstructive surgery. Did I tell my parents I was traveling this weekend? Does anyone know where I am right now? How hard can this guy punch? Will my parents have to take an international flight just to identify the body?

My mind has a tendency to imagine the worst scenarios quickly.

As I am deciding who I want to speak at my funeral, a huge feral grin breaks out across his face as he screams "HAPPINESS!" right along with the song. He hugs me hard enough to nearly shatter my ribs and scream-sings the rest of the song into my face:

> "Happiness seems to be loneliness
> And loneliness chilled my world."

He started singing the lyrics to the song because I looked like I belonged. I fit in. The costume worked!

One of the most terrifying moments of my life turned into one of my greatest memories. There is a smile on my face telling this story right now. "Loneliness" by Tomcraft is still one of my favorite songs.

Before you can ask someone to form an alliance with you, write a guest post on your blog, or have you as a guest on their podcast, you must show that you belong. This is a critical step on the path to earning trust.

You can show that you belong by using the right language, wearing the right clothes and having knowledge about the topics that matter to your audience.

I record a lot of videos in my garden. Before we moved into this house, I recorded all of my videos on the beach in front of our apartment. There are more than a few videos of me walking along the beach and stumbling. When you leave in minor mistakes like that, videos don't feel overproduced. I'm always in the same areas with the same weather, and that consistency shows that these are real videos. That I lead the life I talk about.

If you watch all the videos on my website and social media channels, you can watch me gain and lose weight, grow a beard and shave it, and age. There is no possibility that I recorded these videos on the same day. You will notice that I'm always standing in front of palm trees. That's because all we have in my garden are palm trees and banana trees. My sons are good about killing any flowers that might sneak into our garden, much to my wife's annoyance.

I live on a tropical island, and showing my garden is one of the best ways to prove that I'm living the life I teach about. I'm living my dream life. By recording videos in my garden, I show that I belong.

Last week, someone saw one of my videos and said, "Wow, man, all the surfboards in the background of your videos show that you're the real deal."

I didn't even think about that. I always thought that my surfboards are such an eyesore. I have eighteen surfboards and paddleboards that you can see when I walk around in my videos. Those aren't props, and I didn't place them there to prove anything.

My boards are all of different ages and in different conditions. There are short ones, long ones, paddleboards, and everything in between. There's the board I use when I've got my kids with me, and there's the board I use when I'm by myself. There's the board I use when I'm with my wife, and there's the board I use when I'm trying to learn new moves. There are boards that only my kids can use because I'm too old to learn to use a board that short.

Your life can become your proof in the same way. When I went to castle raves and had a good time without needing to get drunk or enhanced, it showed people that I belonged. I might not have done a certain thing that everyone else was doing, but I was wearing the clothes, listening to the music, and having a good time.

Sometimes you discover your audience, and you go, "Wow. All the people I want to buy my new book hang out on this forum." The very first thing you do is join the forum and post, "Hey, I've got a new book I'm giving away for free for three days." Guess what? They kick you off the forum, and everyone hates you.

One of the fastest ways to get a group of people to hate you is to try to sell something to them without forming any relationship, having a rapport, or showing that you belong. Before you can even think about sales, you must show that you belong there.

Another night out, I was in a club in London called Heaven. That nightclub is more like a cave, and the heat was brutal that night. I am pretty sure that I was sweating all the way through my jeans. It was so hot I thought my heart was going to blow out of my chest. The air conditioning is right next to the ceiling, and hanging from the pipe in front of it, cooling off, is another gorilla. Standing there at five foot nine, I started to wish I was tall enough to reach that pipe.

Suddenly he turns around and looks at me.

Then he looks at his girlfriend.

She's standing right between us, and I can see the wheels spinning in his head.

He stares at me with his beady eyes. He looks at me. Looks at his girlfriend. Looks back at me with malice in those eyes...

I don't know about getting beaten up in London... I start to imaging that it is even worse than getting beaten up in Birmingham. I think. I don't know. I'm going to have to figure out the NHS, how to get new teeth put in, how to get my face fixed.

He looks at me, looks at his girlfriend.

He looks at me.

Looks at the air conditioner.

Looks at me...

Then he picks me up and hangs me from the pipe.

When you show that you belong, people will give you the benefit of the doubt. Instead of making fun of you, trolling you, or kicking you out of their forum or group, they will pick you up and hang you from a pipe in front of an air conditioner so you can cool down at four in the morning at a nightclub in London.

TREAT THEM THE WAY THEY WANT TO BE TREATED

When I was working at that charity in Wales, what those kids wanted was someone who would be there for them and talk to them like they were adults. I can't tell you how many times kids would say to me, "You're the only one that talks to me like a person. Everyone else here talks to me like a child. These other people don't get it."

All the other people who I worked with had never done bad things. They'd never had a drink or a cigarette before, let alone messed around with enhancements. They had never been in a fight, run away from home, or been arrested. They came from good homes.

Yet they were trying to explain things to kids who'd been messing around since they were eleven or twelve years old. They would speak to them in a way that the kids found disingenuous, so they could not move the relationship forward. They didn't understand what these kids wanted. Kids who have grown up lucky, grown up with two parents, grown up loved — they don't understand what it's like.

During my last summer after high school, I became friends with a kid named Justin. We came from opposite sides of the tracks. While I was going off to college with a scholarship, Justin went to work in a slaughterhouse.

His job was killing cows and chopping up meat, one of the toughest jobs you can have, especially in a right-to-work state. The workers can't have a union, can't collectivize, and management treats you pretty badly. I could never do that job.

Sometimes people make the mistake of thinking I look down on blue-collar workers. But when I look upon their work, I tremble with fear. I couldn't do that. I couldn't be a cowboy. I couldn't spend twelve hours a day fixing barbed wire fences or planting fence posts or shearing sheep, let alone cutting cows' throats. I'm just not that tough. I'm very, very lucky.

When he turned eighteen, Justin's parents kicked him out the door with a hearty handshake and a "good luck." He grew up faster than me because he had no choice.

For many of us, going to college is a way to defer adulthood. Kids whose parents kicked them out, checked out, disappeared, or left them, have to grow up faster. So, they see the world differently.

All of my coworkers thought these kids were like them, so they would talk to them like little kids — like they were at fourteen. I said, "No, dude. These kids are tougher than us. These kids have seen things we're afraid of."

When I graduated high school, I realized that most of my friends had been hurt by an adult at some point in their childhood. Out of ten friends, I was the outlier. I was the only kid who had never been hurt by an adult.

I'll be honest; their stories are harrowing. I don't have the right to share them here, but they still haunt me.

Around this time, my father asked me to rank him as a father on a scale of one to ten.

I said, "Well, you've never hurt me or any of my siblings. You're already nine out of ten." The bar is low for parenthood. I think that's something I can't fathom. Yet, so many kids have been through all that bad stuff, and had to grow up fast. They'd had to learn how to survive at an early age.

I gave the kids what they wanted, which was respect. No one wants to be talked to like they're a child. Especially not teenagers who are trying to figure out who they are.

Once you find out who your audience is, you speak to them the way they want to be spoken to. Use their language, act as if you belong, and go where they're hanging out.

GIVE THEM WHAT THEY WANT

My entire business philosophy in life boils down to this: find out what your customers want and then give it to them.

One of my fellow volunteers was invited to play music at a birthday party deep in the valleys of Wales. They invited me to tag along and help set up the equipment. The valleys are quite insular, and it was at a rugby club, because everyone in Wales seems to play rugby.

I had an absolutely fabulous time. I love Wales, in case you hadn't realized. Welsh people are the best, hands down.

When you're DJing in Wales, no matter what genre of music you're playing, you have the best slide in a Tom Jones song. My coworker wisely played a Tom Jones song about three-quarters of the way through his set. At the end of the night, he was winding down the last song and said, "Okay guys, that's the end of the night."

Three local rugby gorillas walked up and said, "You're not going anywhere unless you play a bit of Tom." He says, "I just played a Tom Jones a couple of minutes ago." They responded with, "You haven't played any seventies Tom, now have you?"

Being Welsh himself, my coworker knew what was what, and he had the 1970s Tom Jones record ready to play. He threw it on the turntable—crowd goes wild, night saved. We didn't get beaten up.

Even though they were pretty scary, these gorillas were the best customers you could ever have, because they said what they wanted. They said, "We want a Tom Jones song from the 1970s." You didn't have to guess which of Tom Jones' many wonderful albums to play a song from.

If you listen to your customers, they will tell you what they need — often in the form of complaining, once they're your customers, or aggressively making demands in a rugby club. All you have to do is listen to see what's missing.

There are many ways to find out what your audience wants. By surveying, researching, or getting on the phone with your customers, you can find out what they want. Read all the negative reviews of your competitors to find out what they hate. Your audience is not keeping their desires a secret.

If you want to find out what to write your next romance novel about, look at which romance novels are selling the most. What are the sub-genres? What are people interested in? Which topic on the forum has the most views and most replies? What are people talking about?

The information is there; you just have to look for it. Become a data-driven business, rather than a passion-driven business. It's very easy to say "this is what I want to do", rather than "this is what my customers want me to do."

I can't tell you how many times people have given me something that stinks and then wondered why I don't like them.

If you don't understand what your customers want, you won't have any customers. This can manifest itself in every different type of business model. In order to enter the engagement phase with my audience, I need to get their attention. I need multiple chances to speak to them. There is no better way to do that than through email.

To grow my audience, I give away gifts to everyone I can. I want every visitor to my website, blog, and social media channels to give me their email address, so I offer them a gift in exchange for their contact information. I'm sure you've noticed that I've already written *Give to Get Part 2*. And you can have it for free when you give me your email address. I want to keep speaking to you even after you have finished reading this book.

When you see a gift that matches something you are looking for, you enter your email address and download that gift.

The purpose of that gift is more than getting the email address. Getting your email address is not the end of our relationship; it is the beginning. Don't be tempted to give the bare minimum. What happens when a website gives you a free gift that stinks?

Way too many people give away books that are not books. They are thirteen-page mindmaps and

PDFs of their sales pages—all hype and no content. A real book isn't thirteen pages.

The exchanging of contact details is a critical moment in our relationship, but it's not the end. When I started going to the places that women were going, I discovered that you don't just get someone's phone number and then walk away. You might go, "Okay, I win," and you go back to your buddies to tell them the good news. Then, when you turn around ten minutes later, she's kissing someone better looking on the dance floor. This happened to me a lot because, well, most guys are better looking than me.

You can't treat that initial transaction like it's the end or like you don't have to work hard anymore.

Getting someone's contact details is just the beginning. Keep the conversation going. It has to feel natural. The first phone call is a continuation of that initial conversation, and you have to continue to be cool and interesting.

One time I recorded myself calling a girl on the phone, because I wanted to figure out how I could get better at talking on the phone. I would get a girl's number, and after a single phone call, she would never want to talk to me again. It wouldn't matter how much she liked me at the moment or how good an interaction we'd had. As soon as I called her, it would be dead. I wish I still had this recording, but I lost it many years ago.

At the beginning of the phone call, she was really into me. Two minutes later, she never wanted to speak to me ever again. I said every wrong thing you could: big silence, awkwardness, just the kind of stuff you see in a really awkward romantic comedy.

I played it for my friend Sam to get some advice on how to improve my conversational skills. I said, "Sam, can you tell me what I did wrong?" He listens to it with his mouth drooping open more and more. He just looks at me and goes, "Everything. Maybe you should be a guy who texts."

So now I'm a texter. It's still possible to make a lot of mistakes with texting, but boy, am I bad on the phone! If you're wondering about my wife, we do not do phone calls—we text. Four kids later, Sam was right.

When it comes to giving, go to the extreme: give big, give often, and over-give.

How many times have you walked past a night-club or walked in any major city, and there are people passing out flyers asking you to come to their event? Then you look around, and there are just tons of those flyers on the ground. That's because they've gotten to a place of high traffic, and they're just giving people something they do not want.

You have to give something that matches their needs. If your audience has told you they have a problem, solve it. If you can solve a problem on a single page of a PDF and say, "I've got something that will solve that problem," then people will be grateful for it.

One of my most successful free gifts was a training course on how to cut one of your Internet marketing bills in half. This company would charge you for people that were no longer part of your audience.

o

I said, "Here's what you do. Contact support, then copy and paste this message. They will remove the people they're charging you for who you're not allowed to contact, because those people have left your following. Your bill will go down between fifty and ninety percent. Here's my bill last month, and here's my bill from this month." People loved it.

I solved a very small, specific problem. You don't have to make a huge promise. It's much better to do something small that you could accomplish, and make a promise that you can keep. You just have to find out what people want.

The first free gift I ever created was called "How to Be Good at Kissing." It took me a long time to figure out what I was doing wrong. I've kissed a lot of bad kissers in my life. I said, "Here is how I finally figured it out after the thousands of bad dates, terrible relationships, total debacles, and women who hated me. If a girl kissed me, a girl would kiss anyone. Here is the method."

I was giving it away on my website back when I was teaching about relationships and dating. Guess what? Nobody wanted it, because nobody thinks they are bad at kissing. Between you and me, most people are. It doesn't matter that this amazing guide could have helped so many people. If people think they don't have a problem, they will never want your solution.

If you're giving people something they don't want, they will not move forward in the relationship.

If that boy or girl doesn't want your phone number and doesn't want to give you their phone number, nothing else matters. The relationship won't go any further... until you find out what they want.

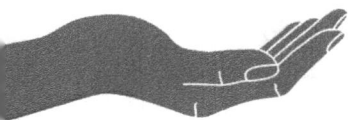

CHAPTER FOUR

Memories are filled based on location. Think back to someone that you worked with for one, two, or even three years, but you only ever saw in the office. If you look at them right now in your mind, how many memories of them do you have?

When I was twenty-four years old, I worked in phone sales for a large computer company. We would sit in this massive room of cubicles, answering phone call after phone call and selling computer after computer. There were some people who I worked with for the entire nine months that I worked there. We spent hundreds of hours side-by-side, yet I only have one or two memories of them. I barely remember them as people.

The people I remember more are the ones I went out to dinner with at different locations. If we went to dinner at five different places, I have five or six memories of them. The more different locations you go to with someone, the more separate memories you'll form.

On my very first date with my wife (who I absolutely hated on our first date and who did not like me either), we went to three different locations. Bar one, bar two, and bar three. Now we're married.

In order to form a relationship, you have to connect with a new person or with your audience in different ways. They have to see you in different environments. And you have to be proactive about pursuing them so that they want to connect with you.

Engagement is a fancy way of saying conversation. The most important thing I can get any new subscriber, follower, or reader to do is reply to one of my emails. If you email me, the odds of us forging a relationship are exponential. It's that important to engage with your audience.

THE LADDER OF TRUST

Most of us are gun-shy when we meet a new salesperson. When you walk onto the car lot, the last thing you want to do is trust the salesperson. As someone who went through car salesman training, I can confirm that the reputation exists for a reason. Their entire goal is to get you to buy a car, whatever it takes.

To overcome the initial skepticism that new customers and business associates feel about you, you must climb the Ladder of Trust. At the bottom of the ladder is a customer who has never heard of you and is completely neutral about your brand. They don't like or dislike you yet.

At each phase in your relationship, you must answer the same question: Does your behavior match their expectation? This can be something as simple as your website loading quickly. As they interact more with your website and online presence, they are continually testing to see if the real you matches who you present yourself as.

Eventually, you'll have enough trust to move from passive to active. The engagement phase begins when a visitor enters their email address on your website in exchange for a gift, and becomes a subscriber. They are now looking to see if you will give them the gift they expected. Do you deliver it fast enough? Does the gift look like it is valuable? Is the content useful? Does the content match the promises you made before they entered their email address?

After they trust you enough to give you their email address, you must build enough trust for them to make a purchase. While you might feel comfortable purchasing my books from a major store, there is a big bridge to get you to make a purchase directly from my website.

In the back of our minds, we all worry that something will go wrong with the transaction, that we won't receive our purchase, or that something sketchy will happen with our payment information.

The price doesn't matter. When a subscriber makes a purchase on your website, they become a customer.

It's critical that they receive what they paid for instantly, feel comfortable with the transaction, and find that the product is worth more than they paid for it.

Once you have a customer, it's a tiny step to sell more expensive products. It doesn't take much more trust to sell a ten-thousand-dollar product than it does to sell a ten-dollar product. After a successful first purchase, your customers will trust your payment process and your ability to deliver a product with a value that matches the promises of your sales page.

The only way to move up the rungs of the Ladder of Trust is to match your potential customer's expectations each time they reach for a new rung. You must give more than they expect at each level, or they will climb no higher.

KEEP YOUR PROMISES

There's nothing worse than letting down your kids. My youngest son is sick right now. He has an infection in his legs that's been persistent for almost two months. Because of that, he can't go into the ocean.

Every time we slip up and let him run into the ocean to play with his older brother and sister, he gets sicker, and it pushes everything back. We have to get more medication and keep him away from the beach longer and longer, and it absolutely stinks.

It breaks my heart every time, because I know what he's going through. When I was a child living in Los Angeles, I got an ear infection that was so bad that they had to put tubes into my ears to drain out whatever was happening inside them. I didn't fully understand. I just knew I was a child having surgery, and I couldn't swim for the entire summer. So, I know how my son feels, and it breaks my heart to disappoint him.

That's how much you should love your customers.

You must keep every promise that you make, no matter how small it seems to you. Because if people don't trust you, they will hate you. How do you feel when you give your email address to a website and the gift never arrives or doesn't solve the problem they promised it would? Are you going to buy something from them in the future?

At every step, you should move the relationship forward. I want you to read every single gift and book I send you. I know that people who consume my gifts like me more than people who don't. My gifts move the engagement phase forward.

If you say, "I'm going to teach you how to lose six pounds in six days," you'd better do it. I once found a website a long time ago, and it said, "I will teach you how to do a hundred pushups in six weeks." I thought, "Yeah, right. This body? I don't think so.

Challenge accepted." Six weeks later, lo-and-behold, I could do a hundred pushups.

I wasn't any stronger; I didn't look any better, but I could do a hundred pushups. He had an entire system of how many to do, when to do them, how many reps—every day for six weeks. And it just worked. It really built up my pushup strength. I'm still talking about that fifteen years later, because he made a single promise, and he kept it.

It's better to make a small promise that you can keep than a big promise that you can't. I remember the first time one of the kids I worked with had a gig DJing. He was so excited he invited all the volunteers to come see him on stage. Everyone said they would be there.

One of my coworkers said, "Wait a minute. Should he even be allowed in a nightclub? He's not eighteen." That's the wrong attitude. That's not going to forge a relationship. The rest of them basically said, "You know what? I don't feel like going. It's not going to be crowded, so let's go where we want to go anyways."

They went to the pub they liked to go to, and I went by myself, because I keep my promises. You have to. If you don't have trust, you have nothing. Do whatever you say you will.

I personally answer every single email. As much as I'd love to have an assistant take over, I can't do that. I answer them all myself. I do it because I have to. It's what I said I would do, which is why you have to be careful with the promises you make.

The first online business I built ten years ago was offering local services. I would help local businesses rank higher in search engines. I told my first clients, "I will help you to be at the top of the charts so you can get more customers. And as part of that, I will be your online internet marketing and digital search engine optimization ninja." Sometimes I would say a "wizard." I would say, "I'm available for you twenty-four seven. Any time you have a question, anytime you're stuck, just call me. I'm always there for you."

Boy, did I learn a lesson! Some of you reading this groaned as soon as you read that, because you know what happened next. People did it. They started calling me all the time.

I had customers who would call me every day and just wanted me to talk to them for hours about what we were working on. At the end of the month, they'd ask, "How come nothing's happened?" I had to say, "Well, I'm always on the phone with you. You won't let me work. I can't work on your project cause I'm on the phone with you."

Some clients were paying me three dollars an hour because they kept me on the phone for so long. It wasn't worth my time. It's hard to change a relationship once you've established it. If someone hires you and you say it's ten dollars an hour, and then one day you say your new price is twenty dollars an hour, they're going to balk. But if they'd met you at the twenty an hour price, it wouldn't be a big deal.

It's a lot easier to find a new client willing to pay the new price than it is to transition an old client to the new promise.

Once you have established a relationship built on a structure of promises, people expect you to meet them. Every time you fail to meet a promise, the value of your relationship with that person goes down. Whereas every time you keep a promise, the relationship stays the same or improves.

Dating is built on a series of promises that climb a Ladder of Trust, just like sales. If you meet someone and have a really good interaction, they might just give you their phone number. Your first date needs to be as fun as that initial interaction, or they will lose interest.

I discovered through my dating misadventures that people will force me to go to boring places and then say the date is boring. All I could say was, "You made me go here. I told you this date would be boring."

I am terrible on dinner dates—most people are. Dinner dates in movies seem amazing; dinner dates in real life are very uncomfortable. They're very awkward. Whenever you're about to have a good connection, the waiter interrupts.

I don't think I've had a successful dinner date in my entire life. I realized that if I met someone at a bar or nightclub and had a great conversation and then said, "Let's go to a dinner date," they would end up hating me. That's because I'm boring at dinners. I'm not good at the conversation. It feels like an interview. It feels awkward and uncomfortable.

But if I instead took her on a tour of all the different art galleries and bars that I liked in my neighborhood, I would have fantastic dates. These are places where I'm comfortable, and I can be interesting. I can maintain the promise—the promise to be interesting.

Sometimes promises are implicit. If you're fun on the first date, you should be fun on the second date. If someone reads the first book in your series and you change the genre in book two, people will hate you.

I read a series of books where the author did that, and every time I see one of his new books, I don't just have a neutral response. I have a negative response. In book five in a series about space marines, this author changed to a heavy-handed political genre. The marines stopped fighting aliens and started fighting civilian humans. No, thank you.

You can't do that. You can't inject politics this late in the game. You can't do that. You have to do that from book one or start a new series. If you switch genres on me, I'm going to stop reading your books.

Something tells me you've been on a good first date with someone, and then the second date was terrible. Or maybe the third or the fourth date. The person didn't keep their promises.

Sometimes their personality changes or you start to realize that they're not exactly who you thought they were. Or you're not what they thought you were. That's why most relationships end.

I've only ever had one successful relationship in my entire life; that's the one with my wife. Every other relationship ended. This is the only one that hasn't ended yet. Hopefully, it will never end.

If you promise that your gift will solve a problem, it has to. If you promise that if I swing by your mechanic shop or gas station, you will inflate the air in my tires for free, you must do that. Whenever you promise anything, whether it's implicit or explicit, hidden in the message or said straight up, you have to do it.

People do not want free gifts from people they don't like or trust. Once you break trust with someone, it's nearly impossible to get back. It's honestly better to start over, try to find someone else, and just not break your promise with the next person.

THE FIRST PROMISE

1. ANCHORED VALUE

It's important to establish a strong relationship with anyone who enters your email list, and giving them as much value as possible is the best way to do that.

When I was planning this book, I wanted to give so much value that readers felt inspired to take action. I didn't want to write a book that doesn't work, doesn't inspire people, or is missing steps. I wanted to create a guide that you can use to create your very own Extreme Giving business.

In your business, you want to create pivots. A pivot is a powerful tool that you can use to leverage your entire business into success. It is a resource that you can use in multiple ways to grow your business. A great pivot can turn into the fulcrum for your entire business.

One of the greatest pivots for an Extreme Giving business is a book. Books have anchored value. When you give away a gift that people are buying somewhere else, then the gift has value anchored in the real world. They can see exactly what the gift is worth. It's like leaving the receipt in the box of a present.

If you see a free book on my website, you don't know if it's any good or has any value - until you read it. But if you see that same book in a bookstore for ten dollars, the value suddenly becomes real. Real people have paid actual money for that book and then left positive reviews.

If I say you can buy the hardback edition of a book for $24.99 or download the digital edition for free, it has real value. The book would have even more value if it had reviews (which it should), because people would then be able to see verification of its value.

You can tell me that your gift is worth ninety-seven dollars, but if no one has ever paid that price, then there is no anchored value. A free gift without anchored value is not worth anything. You only perceive it as having value because of smoke and mirrors.

A book has value if people have paid for it and were pleased with what they bought. The more anchored value something has, the more people can understand that they're getting something useful and valuable, the happier they're going to be, and the easier it will be to make a profit.

When you're giving something away or asking for someone's email address, you want to give them something great. That's why I am a big believer in giving someone an amazing book.

By giving them something that they can buy elsewhere, they're able to see exactly how much that gift is worth, and that's an Extreme Gift.

2. SOLVE A PROBLEM

Not everyone has the time to write and publish a book just in order to give it away. If your gift doesn't have anchored value, it must solve a measurable problem. After someone consumes and implements your gift, they should be able to say whether it worked or not.

Your free book doesn't have to be long; it just has to make the reader's life better.

I have a friend who once said that he would pay more money for a one-page PDF that taught him a really cool trick to make more money, than he'd pay for a five-hundred-page book that taught him every step on how to make money.

Brevity has value in and of itself. If you give people something valuable, even if it's small, then you can start that relationship on the right foot. That is why my guide showing people how to lower their internet bills was such a massive success. If your back hurts right now, and I can show you a five-minute stretch that makes the pain go away, you're going to love me. You won't complain that the gift was too small.

When you're trying to solve a problem, it doesn't have to be big. If you can give people a quick win, such as how to lose one pound in one hour, how to cut their bill in half, or how to hire a new writer, you're going to keep their attention. People want to see quick results, and if you can give that to them, they'll trust you more. And if they trust you more, they'll move up that Ladder of Trust and be one step closer to becoming a paying customer.

3. EMAIL ADDRESSES ARE EXTREMELY VALUABLE

An email address is precious. It's private, personal, and valuable, and it's one of the most critical elements of the Extreme Giving model.

The customer journey is the path people take to find you, buy your products, and interact with you after that purchase.

Many people mistakenly think the customer journey starts when a customer pulls a credit card out of their wallet. But I consider the gift to be the first step along this journey, because they're paying for your Extreme Gift with their email address. While they're not giving you money, they're giving you their personal information, which is worth so much more than the price of a book.

For many of us, email addresses are more valuable than money. I would rather pay seven dollars to never get an annoying email ever again, than save that money and have my inbox cluttered with forwards and updates that I'll never read.

I want you to realize that the fulcrum of the entire Extreme Giving system is to give people something of true value as a way to thank them for their email addresses. You're saying that you respect them and that you treasure having personal access to them.

I only give away things that are magical, valuable, and wonderful, because I want you to know how much you mean to me. We're bartering and creating a relationship, and this is how you start a powerful relationship.

If you cut corners on this step and give away something that isn't valuable, you start that relationship off on the wrong foot, and we don't want to do that.

It's critical that the product you use as the fulcrum with your Extreme Giving business is worth what you say it's worth. Your gift isn't free; it should be worth an email address, and that has an entirely different economic value.

I BELIEVE IN YOU

During my year of charity, I clearly remember the first time a kid came up to me with hope in their eyes and said, "I want to do this, but I don't think I can." Parents or teachers didn't believe in them, and they didn't think they had what it took. This happened so many times over that year of my life, whether it was kids who wanted to go to college, kids who wanted to have a career, or kids who wanted to do something more than live off the state's dollar.

These kids wanted to work and make something of themselves. They had dreams and hopes, but they'd been told so many times that they weren't good enough. I know what that feels like, because people have said it to me.

When I was in my freshman year of high school, I was on the soccer team. I did my best, but I was the backup goalie, and I never thought I was going to get into the game. The starting goalie was a natural athlete, and I assumed he would play every minute of every game for the entire season.

And then he got hurt in the middle of a game, so everything changed.

My dad walked up to me and said, "You're going in; I think his arm is broken." I said, "What? Don't even joke." My dad pulled me off the bench, grabbed a soccer ball, and warmed me up. Then the coach put me in.

I went into the game and *saved* the game. I had my magical high school moment, my moment.

It was one of those spectacular moments that meant so much to me, and the rest of the team has probably forgotten. I made the big save.

After some X-rays, we found out that the starting goalie was out for the season. I was the only goalie left on the team.

My coach never believed in me. He felt that I would never be good enough, because I'm not a natural athlete. I didn't look like an athlete, and it didn't matter how hard I worked.

He said, "You can't be the goalie; you're not tall enough." In my head, I thought, "Now I understand why this guy in his sixties is still coaching the freshman soccer team and can't get a varsity job at any school in the entire city." Even the schools with terrible teams wouldn't hire him, and I'd figured out why—because his mind was small.

For the rest of the season, he took this kid, Doug, and put him in every single game. Doug was taller than me and very, very clumsy.

First game: Doug plays the first half, and the other team scores four goals. In the second half, I go in. With the same number of shots made toward a goal, they score only one goal on me. This was consistent throughout the season. Statistically, I was four times better than Doug—but Doug was taller than me.

Each game, the coach would put me in less and less, and every single game, we would lose by more and more.

In the last game of the season, we were playing against our rivals from the other private school. Doug was in the goal. For the first half of the game, two players stood on either side of Doug, heading out as many goals as they could. They would jump in and head the ball out, hoping to save the game.

In the first half, Doug let in a barrage of goals, and we were getting destroyed. I stood up to play the second half as I'd been doing for the season. The coach turned and said no. He said, "No, you're not going in Doug's place. He's playing both halves." I can't put in this book what I said to that coach, but I belittled him in every single way I knew how.

As a fifteen-year-old, I said a lot of curse words. In the mix of all the bad words, I explained that his terrible coaching is why he was still coaching freshmen in his sixties… "Doug is terrible. You should put in the player who can block the most goals, not the one you like the most. We'll never win another game as long as you keep doing this."

And we never did. That coach did not believe in me, and it was devastating.

I stopped playing soccer, because I realized it did not matter to him how good I was, how many goals I stopped, or what I achieved. He'd made a decision that I didn't have what it took, so I would never be allowed to play. That terrible coach was the one to choose who got to play and who didn't.

So, I pivoted.

For high school, I dug deeper into martial arts instead, and I qualified for the Junior Olympics. I was also on the school's debate team—one of the debate teams with the most wins in the history of the United States. I have so many trophies because my debate and martial arts coaches believed in me. That's the difference.

When you don't believe in someone, you can devastate them. These children I encountered, people didn't believe in them much, other than their soccer skills. They frequently heard, "You'll never get a job. You'll never amount to anything. You'll never matter." That's brutal.

You can transform a life just by saying, "You matter." Sometimes I didn't even have to say that. When you're working with children with no hope, sometimes all you have to do is listen. That can be enough to be transformative. They go, "Wow, you listen to what I have to say. You don't interrupt me. You don't give me advice. You make me feel like a person and like an adult." And then they start to believe they have significance.

That's how you create a friendship. That's how you form a relationship with your audience. It doesn't matter if it's through an email list, a Rolodex of customers, people you send postcards to, a social media following, or however we communicate in the future—with virtual reality or androids. Once people are communicating with you, and you have entered the relationship's engagement phase, if you believe in them more than the competition, they will want to hang out with you.

My soccer story isn't over quite yet.

As I was coming off the field, my father heard what I said to the coach. It terrified me, because this was the first time he had heard me say bad words, especially to an adult and an authority figure. I thought, "Oh no, I've broken the ultimate taboo."

Not only was this person an adult, but they were also a teacher. He was a coach. He had authority over me, and I showed a complete and total lack of respect.

My dad says, "You're not supposed to talk to adults like that, but I can't punish you, because you're right. He's a full bird..." And then my dad said a bad word of his own. It might have been the first time I'd ever heard my dad call someone a bad word, and it blew my mind.

Which do you want to follow? Who do you want in your corner? You can choose who you follow. Do you want to follow the person who believes that you will accomplish great things or the person who says you'll probably never make it?

Do you want to follow my freshman soccer coach? Or do you want to follow my dad, the one who backs you up when the going gets tough? Do you want the person who says you're capable of anything and who believes in you? That's who you need to be, because that's an amazing type of person to be. It's a place of great generosity. It allows Extreme Giving to be easy.

I implement Extreme Giving throughout my business because I believe in you. If I didn't believe in you, I wouldn't have asked you to read this book. I would not invite you to my training sessions. I would not share free videos and blog posts with you. I would not put so much content out there in front of you, because I'd be wasting your time.

I am not an entertainer. That's not my role in our relationship. I believe in you, and I wouldn't put educational and transformative materials in front of you if I didn't think they would work. That would make me a monster.

Do you understand that? Think about that for a moment—the type of person who would sell someone a product that they don't think works. I've had someone do that to me, and I would never do it to someone else. That haunts me.

Ten years ago, when I first started getting into this business, I got in a lot of trouble because I called out some people who were selling things that were unethical. I said something so publicly in an old blog post that people reached out to me and asked me to take it down. I said, "If you can point to a single sentence in this post that is untrue, I will delete the entire post." They did not reply.

I cannot work with or abide by people whose products don't work. I cannot work with people who don't back up their products. I cannot work with people who don't provide this same level of support that I do. Because I believe in you.

To succeed in this business, you have to believe in what you're selling, and you have to believe in your customers. When I'm recommending a course, I say, "This program is great if you want to learn this."

I don't know how to do everything, so I find someone who's an expert. I say, "If you really want to learn e-commerce, you can't learn from me—it's not what I do. But here's someone who's an expert, and I trust them. I examined their course; it's rock-solid. I've looked at other students who've been through it and had success."

If someone emails me asking if they should buy a program, about eighty percent of the time, the answer is no. Because I get paid a commission, I am losing money every time I say no. Yet that's my answer, because I care, and this isn't the right program for you.

If you're on the fence and these are your questions, or you can't quite afford it, or you have to split it between two credit cards, don't do it. It's not the right time for you. But don't worry. There'll be another opportunity that is the right one for you.

That's how my journey started. I bought a program that I couldn't afford. It was five hundred dollars a month for six months, and I had five hundred dollars left before I could max out my credit. I scraped together the first payment, and for the next six months, I had to earn five hundred a month just to make the payments.

I know what it's like to be on the edge—to be all in. That program transformed my life.

One course can change your life, because that's what happened to me. I went all in on it. But it has to be the right program for you, at the right time. Because I believe in you, I want to fit you with what's right for you. If you hate the sound of your voice, I will not teach you how to podcast. If you have dyslexia, I will not force you to write a book, because it's not the right fit for you.

I want you to have success.

How do you feel knowing that I believe in you? Doesn't it make you want to read the next page? Read my next book?

Now, think about how your customers and potential customers could feel if they knew you believed in them.

Do you think they would read your next email? Absolutely. Do you think they would want to connect with you? Absolutely. Do you think if you asked them to test your new product, come to your events or introduce you to someone else who they think would be a great fit for what you do, would they do that? Of course they would!

It's great to be surrounded by people who like us. It's even better to be surrounded by people who believe in us.

KEEP THEM INTERESTED

When I was in my late twenties, I was friends with a guy and a girl. The girl was in love with the guy. The guy was very aware of it, but he had no feelings for her. She was so into him, but she was passionate about a caricature. She was obsessed with a person that didn't even exist.

When we have a massive crush on a person, it's our imagination of the person, not who they are, that we have feelings for. I will never forget when she said, "He still has feelings for me. He says he doesn't like me. He says he hates me, and he says I'm annoying. Hatred isn't the opposite of love—indifference is."

That stuck with me, because that's an intense thing to say. Indifference is a powerful word. There is nothing worse than someone feeling indifferent about you. Fear of indifference caused many of the children I interacted with in the program to act out. Not because they were bad, but because they craved attention. Negative attention is better than no attention.

My son is four years old, and he will act out and then smile. Because he knows he's guilty, but at least I'm looking at him. I try to give my kids as much love and attention as I possibly can, but they always want more.

When my son does something bad, he doesn't hide. He doesn't run away. He's right there looking at me in the eye, because he feeds off that attention. Yet, there are so many children in the system, who no one cares about anymore. They're the victims of indifference. They're forgotten.

You cannot let that enter your relationship with your audience. This means that you can never be boring. If you're boring, the indifference will flow in the other direction.

If I told you that I'm going to send you ten emails over the next ten days, and nine of them will be boring while only one will be interesting? Would you open all ten? You might open one, two, or even three, hoping the interesting one comes in the first couple of days. But if it doesn't, I'm going to lose you.

There are a lot of ways that you can be interesting. I know so many people who have launched podcasts and didn't start making a living from them for eight, nine, even ten years. That's a really long time.

They didn't see their podcast as part of a larger structure. I don't see a podcast as a business in and of itself unless you're in the entertainment industry, then it's possible. In our field, there's so much more. My podcast is just a part of my business. My podcast serves one purpose: engagement.

I used to put out five episodes a week before I got sick. I put out 160 solo episodes until I got so sick and couldn't do it anymore. Now I do a weekly episode. I wish I could do more.

I'm so passionate about my podcast, but it doesn't generate any revenue. It serves a single purpose: to keep my audience interested between books. This book is the hardest book I've written. Three times I've torn down everything and started over from zero because it wasn't right.

The first version was the wrong message. The second version was all teaching, but it was boring. I committed the very sin that I'm telling you about right now. A member of my team read the book, and she said, "This doesn't even feel like you wrote it; it's so boring." And I was like, "Oh no. That's the worst possible thing you could say."

Anytime you have an inkling—if you are thinking that something might be boring, might be offensive, or there might be something wrong with it—that's how everyone else will feel. If you're on the fence, everyone else will feel that way. That's exactly what she thought, and she was right.

I committed the ultimate crime. The book was educational and I had all this amazing information in it, but it was boring. It didn't have enough stories, and it didn't have enough of me. The last thing I want within our relationship is indifference. The training part of that book was amazing, but it didn't have all the personal stories that have kept you engaged with me this deep into the book.

You can show your audience you are not indifferent about them by believing in them. Make sure they don't become indifferent about you. You must be interesting.

This means you have to consistently generate high-quality content. You have to respond to your followers, and you have to meet them where they are. If your audience needs videos, you need to record videos.

If your audience only likes podcasts, you need to provide podcast content. If your audience wants blog posts, you need to provide blog posts. If your audience only wants books, provide books. However you need to engage with your audience, engage with them.

Engagement can be the bridge between purchases for whatever type of business you're in. Whether you're selling shoes or you're a lawyer, you want to stay in your audience's mind as long as possible. That way, when they need your service or their next pair of shoes, you're where they go because you're the first one they think of.

You can see businesses like accountant firms trying to stay on your mind with their weekly newsletters.

They are doing it wrong, but at least they're trying. They're attempting to stay top-of-mind. They send out what they consider topical information like the monthly tax updates, and they tell you when things are due. The emails are unbelievably boring, but boring is better than nothing, right? I'd rather you think of me as boring than not think of me at all.

You want to create a lasting friendship, and it's a simple three-step process. Keep your promises, believe in your audience, and then keep them interested. **That's all** it takes to climb the Ladder of Trust.

I'm trying to expand my social media following, and that means I'm recording more videos than ever before. It's a lot of work to keep your social channels active. You have to post multiple times every day if you want to appear at the top of your followers' feeds.

Feeds are organized by recency and relevance. Nobody is going to see your post from three days ago when they log in.

If they log in right after I've made a post, they'll see my post. On social media, frequency leads to more engagement. You can get away with a podcast once a week, once every two weeks, once a month—but once a day isn't enough for most social media channels.

People are voracious, so you have to put out content three, four, or five times a day on each channel. The method of communication you're using with your audience determines how frequently you have to put out content. Whatever you can do to strengthen the relationship with your audience, do it.

Show that you care about them and be interesting. When you're interesting, it shows you care, because you're meeting them where they want to be met. You're talking about things they find interesting.

The first two versions of this book were the versions that I wanted to write. This is the version you want to read, because I'm creating something that you find interesting. It tells you I care about you; it creates engagement, and it creates a relationship.

Good engagement allows us to move into phase three of our business, because Extreme Giving is absolutely how I pay every one of my bills. It's the phase I'm sure you're the most excited about: profit.

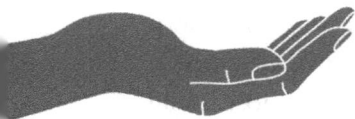

CHAPTER FIVE

When it comes to a for-profit business, the only number on the scoreboard that matters is profit. It is the most accurate measure of success. Profit is how much money you get to keep after all of your expenses.

When I was working for the charity, money was not the measure of success. My coworkers measured success by how much they liked each other, how strong their friendships were, and how much they enjoyed their meetings.

My measurement of success was how many children would ask me deep questions about life, religion, and hope. The more eyes I could put light into, the more I mattered. That's why my path deviated from my coworkers so much: They cared about the journey, while I cared about the result.

Last year we tried to hire a new manager inside my company. For the first two weeks, she held meeting after meeting. She would have meetings with everyone, talk to them, get to know them.

She was really passionate about relationships and connections.

She knew more about my employees' personal lives and feelings than I did. She really connected with them and figured out what their needs were and where they were in their careers. She did all these wonderful things—and revenue was plummeting. I said to her, "We're a business. If we don't bring in more money than we spend on salaries, someone's going to get fired."

A few days later, she quit. She didn't want to work for a business where there was pressure on her to generate revenue just so we could meet salaries. She didn't want to work for a company where her work actually mattered.

I was confused, because I've always thought this is how a successful business operates. I've never heard of a company that doesn't care if their employees cost more money than they generate.

I pay my team every single weekend.

I look at my books every single week and ask myself, "Did we make more money this week than last week? Did we make more money this week than we're spending?"

I don't look at what happened last week. We might have had a massive profit last week, but I don't carry that over, because I'm trying to perform every single week. That's the standard I hold myself to.

I don't think the size of the company matters: Do you want an employee who feels like there should be no connection between their work and the profit coming in? How about the manager for the entire team?

It was a good decision for our manager to quit. She wasn't in alignment with our company culture; we want to make enough money to pay everyone. If you can't get into alignment with that core concept, you should not apply for a job here.

Money does not appear by magic, even though my children think it does. They think the ATM is a magic money machine. Every dollar comes from the sweat of my brow. I've already almost completely sweat through the shirt I'm wearing while dictating this chapter.

Hard work generates profit, and I work just as hard as the members of my team to make sure that every single week they always have the money that they need to pay their bills.

CUSTOMERS SHOULD FEEL SPECIAL

Every single person on your mailing list should wake up excited to see what you have put in their mailbox today. They should have that Christmas morning feeling each time they open one of your emails or click one of your links. Fill your emails with engaging content, cool gifts, and as much value as possible. With every communication channel, our goal is to create the Entourage Effect.

Everyone on my mailing lists knows that I run two book giveaways every month. That knowledge means they will be more forgiving when I send them an email that misses the mark. Rather than unsubscribe, they will give me another chance. They will stick around longer, because they know more gifts are headed their way. The Entourage Effect earns me additional grace from my subscribers.

This also gives you more breathing room and more time for improvement. If some of your content isn't that great, or if one of your lessons or products isn't exactly a hit with your audience, you can fix it.

At best, ten percent of my audience responds strongly to each course, training, or book that I share with them. It's nearly impossible to come up with something that every single person who follows me will want to read, download, or purchase. Rather than try to appeal to everyone with every email, I rotate through interests. While today's email might not be your cup of tea, if you stick around for a few weeks, one of my emails will be perfect for you.

Different people respond to different things. Some people really want to sell physical products, some want to be authors, and some want to learn about email marketing. I try to meet everyone's needs. Sometimes, you're going to hear about programs, courses, or books that just don't appeal to you. That's okay. As long as you know that something good is coming around the corner, you won't jump ship as quickly as you would from the list of someone who never provides value to you.

If someone gives just enough value to get you on their mailing list, you're going to jump ship the first time they mess up or suggest something that doesn't appeal to you. You abandon ship, unsubscribe from their emails, and you're gone forever.

Extreme Giving allows me to give enough value to avoid that calamity.

In exchange for value, what I really want from my audience is grace. I want them to forgive me if I make a mistake, stay on my list if they get an email they don't understand, or talk to me if they buy a product from me that doesn't work. I want them to email me and ask me to fix it, rather than call their credit card company.

If a product doesn't work or doesn't arrive when it should, I want my followers to give me the benefit of the doubt and assume that it was just a mistake that I can fix.

Mary E. said, "I think the primary reason I follow you and read your emails is because you always read mine and respond to them. Sometimes, a link doesn't work, and I let you know right away, and you always show me your thanks... I appreciate that."

I want every customer to have the same experience as Mary.

I answer every email that you send to me, and I always take care of the issue. Sometimes, I redirect it to my support team or tech team so they can deal with it more quickly, but I always make sure it gets sorted out. That's just a part of the journey.

The longer you stay with me, the more value you get.

I received a message last week on one of my Skype channels from someone who purchased a coaching package from me about four years ago. When he asked to have a one-on-one phone call with me next week, I was happy to oblige, because I still want him to succeed. He hasn't paid me a single penny in over three years, but that doesn't matter. I'm still rooting for him.

That's the value you get when you're on a journey with me, and that's the value your audience should get when they're on a journey with you. They should know that the best is yet to come, whether they've been following you for one week or for ten years.

MONEY SHOULDN'T CHANGE ANYTHING

When visitors, subscribers, and fans spend their first dollar with you, they transition into customers. They have reached the top of the Ladder of Trust. You have built up enough creditability with them for them to give you some of their hard-earned money.

Everyone has a different trust threshold, and some people will make a purchase on their very first visit to your website. Others need to spend months in the engagement phase. They take longer to bring up the Ladder of Trust.

Rather than jump people right to the top of the Ladder of Trust, we let them take baby steps. We allow visitors to climb one rung at a time, giving them a chance to get to know us. I'm not afraid to earn your trust. We start with consistency and solid content. Eventually, visitors to my website feel comfortable enough to enter their email addresses and download my gifts.

It takes even more trust for them to enter payment information for a product. A new customer must feel comfortable enough with your website to enter their most personal details. They must believe that they will get the product they've ordered in a reasonable timeframe and that the product will match your promises. They must also believe that if there's a problem, your customer support team will respond in a timely manner and offer them a refund if the product fails to meet their expectations.

Earlier this year, a glitch developed in between my shopping cart and membership area. For six weeks, when you bought one product from me, you would get immediate access to that product and my membership area. However, if you bought a second product, whether five minutes or six months later, you would not get access until we manually granted it. We had to log into our sales dashboard several times a day, to see if any purchases had come in. Sometimes, people would have instant access to their first purchase, but they wouldn't have access to their second purchase until six hours later.

I'm describing a terrible customer experience, and it frustrated me the entire time. When people try to buy something and don't get timely access, they get enraged; some support emails came in calling us a scam or a rip-off.

I couldn't blame them, because I feel the same way when I have to wait days to get access to a purchase. If it's not immediate, I assume that I've been tricked.

I spent an insane number of hours with three different tech support teams that spent more time blaming each other than trying to solve the problem. My shopping cart team blamed my membership area, my membership area team blamed my hosting company, and my hosting company blamed the other two. In the end, I had to pay a lot of money to a specialist to fix the problem.

If you buy something from me and don't receive what you purchased in a timely fashion, you don't care about my tech problems. You just want your product, not excuses.

When you enter the profit phase, you must continue to build on the trust that got you there. If you put in all that effort to bring a customer to the buying decision only to hand them a product that doesn't meet their expectations, all of your effort will have been wasted. They will ask for a refund, and the bridge will burn.

When a visitor gives you their email address, it's not the end of the hard work. And the same applies to the first purchase. It's your job to maintain and build on that relationship, so your customers come back again and again. Money isn't the end of the Ladder of Trust; now, you have to keep your customers at the top.

Extreme Giving must energize every part of your business. It will ensure you never even desire to cut corners or sell a shoddy product just to make ends meet. When you truly embrace this mindset, hard decisions become easy. You will always know the right thing to do.

THE RECOMMENDATION

At the charity cafe, there was one child who was more reticent than the rest. She seemed to have the most problems, and we all struggled to find a way through her shell. She refused to open up to any of the workers. Far too many children come from a place where the people they should be able to trust the most are the people they trust the least.

Children can lose trust in all adults and authority figures when they come from a home where the parents don't meet their needs, aren't there for them, or are indifferent. If parents do harm to children, and then those children go to a school where the teachers don't notice, they're going to stop trusting adults.

Everyone at the cafe would try to crack this nut. All the other workers thought, "If we could just help this one child..." "If we could connect with this one person..." That's the panacea, right? We always want to climb the highest mountain.

In the words of Sir Edmund Hillary, the first person to summit Mount Everest, "I did it because it was there." Everyone wanted to make a difference with that most reticent of the kids who came into our cafe, but she wouldn't open up to anyone.

I noticed that she was connecting with other kids. Some of the kids she opened up to were the same kids that I had seen outside of work hours. They had a little more engagement with me than the other workers, and that became my bridge to this young lady.

One of the other kids finally said to her, "Hey, you can talk to Jonathan. He's cool", which is the ultimate recommendation from a teenager.

I'm going to let you in on a little secret: I'm not cool. I've never been cool. I tried hard for many years to get there, but I wasn't ever cool. But a teenager gave me his stamp of approval, and she opened up to me. She opened up about what she was going through, and I was able to help her - just by listening.

You can only do so much when you have limited power. But at least we could provide a place where she felt safe. From one "he's cool" from a teenager, we got her access to the support she needed from the right people. Because one kid recommended me, I was then able to recommend people I trusted to her.

The most powerful weapon in your arsenal is the recommendation, and I use this in every area of my business.

I met my wife through a recommendation. A business partner of mine was going on a date, and his date was bringing a friend. He brought me along to meet the friend and said, "I recommend you to each other." Now we're married.

It's much harder to walk up to a stranger in a bar and strike up a conversation than to have a friend introduce you. That simple introduction gives you a foundation to build on and bypasses a great deal of awkwardness. You don't have to start the Ladder of Trust at zero.

I build most of my revenue on a foundation of recommendations. The products I recommend generate far more revenue than the products I create. My audience trusts my recommendations because of the trust between us.

I believe in my audience, so I'm very careful to only recommend products that pass through my vetting process. If a customer has a problem with a product, they'll often reach out to my support team rather than the product's support team. My audience knows that I'm in their corner. If they aren't getting the support they deserve, then I'll directly message that product owner. I bypass the red tape. I don't have to deal with the five-dollar-an-hour support staff. I go straight to the top, and that's powerful.

I work with a broker named Mike. He represents forty other affiliates like me, who recommended products that they believe in. He vets a product and brings it to me, and then my team vets it again. Mike gets paid a percentage of every sale I generate, by the product owner.

Because Mike represents forty people like me, he has a lot more leverage than I do.

If you have a problem with a purchase, the product owner's support team might blow you off because you're just a single individual consumer. When you reach out to me, I speak with the authority of my entire audience. If that's not enough, I can reach out to Mike, who will reach out to them with the authority of forty times my power. That's a lot of juice.

Just knowing that Mike is in my corner and that I'm in your corner gives you more trust to make purchases. I'm transferring the trust I built during the engagement phase to the product I recommend. That part of you that wonders whether you'll get a refund if the product doesn't match expectations gets additional support. Instead of hoping that this new company honors their refund policy, you know that Mike and I will make them.

Mike's recommendation holds a lot of weight. If he tells me not to promote something, then I don't promote it. If he tells me to promote something, I'm going to give it a hard look. I don't promote every single thing he recommends to me, but he has a good feel for what my audience will respond to.

While selling only your own products is wonderful, it is also a lot of work. Many successful companies were built through recommendations. The shelves of the biggest stores in the world are lined with products made by other companies.

One of the best ways to find what your audience likes is to recommend products you think might be a good fit. Then watch the sales numbers. They will buy what they want, and that can help you plan what to recommend or create next.

I give away free books to people on my mailing list all the time. I love hosting Extreme Giving events. I have events all the time. After you take a free book for me, I ask what types of books you want in the future. Tell me the authors to approach for my next book giveaway.

Every year I reach out to hundreds of authors. I want to put their message in front of my audience. The tighter the match between book and audience, the better.

Besides asking about what types of books you want, I also ask for a piece of hard data. What was the last thing you purchased online? How much did it cost?

Data about a purchase is far more valuable than opinion. People tell me books that interest them, but they would never buy, all the time. It's easy to say you like something, but voting with your credit card is the real deal. When you spend actual money, it moves from the realm of opinion to fact.

Build up a pool of products you feel comfortable recommending. You can make a living from your opinions. You will get paid a commission for your recommendations from the product owners, while you gather data on what your audience wants and needs.

Asking people if they would buy something doesn't give accurate data. Most people will give the answer they think you want. They want to avoid hurting your feelings. The only vote that really matters is the purchase. That's true customer behavior.

The easiest way to get to this hard data is to show your audience products that you find interesting. I curate products that I think might be a good fit for my followers. When I give a recommendation, I'm saying that I think this program, course, or tool is going to meet their needs.

If you like the recommendation, buy it. If you don't, that's okay too.

My job is not to sell you anything. My job is to put things in front of you that you might find interesting.

People will give these products more attention because it's your recommendation. Not only are they more likely to buy a product because you've recommended it, but you've also given it your seal of approval. You've said, "Hey, this product's pretty cool." You'll also get paid if they buy it, and you'll learn what your audience wants to buy.

I've dramatically changed my business over the past year, by paying more attention to what my audience responds to. The recommendation can transform your business. It transfers the trust, rapport, and relationship your customer has with you into whatever product you're recommending. Therefore, it's important to only recommend things you believe in.

TRACK AND IMPROVE

Despite my best efforts, sometimes my foot ends up in my mouth. It happens to the best of us. Sometimes you just say the wrong thing.

One of my coworkers was having a conversation with a new kid in the cafe when I saw this happen in slow motion. Time slowed down as I watched a conversation turn into a car crash. Less than five minutes after the kid walked through the door, my coworker said, "Hey, what's going on between you and God? What's your jam here?"

She tried to do it in a cool, hip way—the kind of way dads use to try to be cool. I'm very familiar with "dad cool," as I'm creeping into my forties and entering the dad-joke phase of my life. My days of teenagers calling me cool are now in the rearview mirror.

I watched the conversation crumble, because she went for the sale way too soon. The kid started pulling the red "eject" lever repeatedly, thinking, "I've got to get out of this conversation. Just another overbearing adult, trying to force their paradigm (whether it's religion or politics or beliefs, whatever) on top of me, and I don't have time for that. I get enough of that from everyone else."

My coworker wasn't listening. You can learn from your mistakes, and you can learn from other people's mistakes. It's better to learn from other people's mistakes. That's what you're doing by reading this book.

I'm teaching you a business that I've forged over ten years. I made a lot of mistakes along the way. Reading this book allows you to bypass those mistakes by learning from mine. You don't have to learn the hard way.

If you can implement this Extreme Giving concept within your business, your business will be recession-proof, pandemic-proof, election-proof. If you can forge these types of relationships with your customers, your business will continue, and it will go the distance.

You're receiving data all the time. Are you paying attention?

Physical stores are far more guilty of a lack of attention than digital stores. If you own a brick-and-mortar business and you're reading this book, that's outstanding. This can absolutely be transformative for your business.

Let me ask you a few questions:

How many people walked through your store today?

How many of them made a purchase?

How many of them didn't?

What was the average order value?

I watch these shows all the time where they bring in a business wizard to ask the same questions. What are your best-selling products? What are your worst-selling products? Get rid of the worst-selling ten percent of products and put in more of your best 10 percent. Surprise—you're making more money. It's revelatory for so many businesses, because they're gathering data, but they're not paying attention to it.

One revelation I had in my business that transformed my revenue is that it is just as hard to sell something for three hundred dollars as it is for three thousand. I want you to think about that for a moment. It's just as hard to walk someone through either product. It's the same amount of work, except you make ten times more money.

It took me nine years to learn that lesson. I'm giving you a massive shortcut. I'd heard it many times and never really believed it. I only changed when I looked at my data and began running tests.

To confirm my hypotheses, we ran two recommendation campaigns back to back. One product was two thousand dollars, and the other was five hundred. We sold almost the same number of units of both, except one campaign made four times more money.

Listen to your audience. They're telling you what they want and what they need.

As you interact with your audience, you need to track and improve the metrics that matter.

Last year a potential employee bragged to me that his online magazine had a reach of four million people. I wasn't familiar with this metric. I didn't know what reach meant.

Reach is an imaginary metric. Reach is how many people could possibly see your message. If you print four million copies of a newspaper, your reach is four million. That doesn't mean someone is going to read every copy. Maybe nobody will read it.

Don't get distracted by false metrics. Potential is not measurable; therefore, it's not a real metric

The real metric is how many people interact with your communications.

I'm in the middle of a campaign to expand my Facebook page right now. I know a lot of my audience spends time on this platform, so I want to connect with them. As part of this process, I'm posting videos and quotes and memes every day. Social media is voracious, and I need to post different types of content multiple times a day if I want to capture my audience's attention.

That's the critical metric. I want to know how many people played the video, clicked the like button, or left a comment. I look at which types of videos they're responding to. Do they like emotional videos, or do they like educational videos? Short videos, or long videos? What types of subjects do they respond to the most?

When a video gets a lot of engagement, I make more videos like it. By looking at what my customers respond to and acting on it, I can increase my engagement every week.

The recommendations that generate the most revenue should become your priority. If you recommend ten products in a row and number nine has the best sales, you need to change the order. New followers should hear about number nine first.

Your most successful recommendation should become your first recommendation for new customers.

I have a large list of tools I recommend on the Toolbox page of my website. The listings at the top with the largest images aren't my favorite products— they are my audience's favorites. The products that generate the most sales move to the top of the page.

I believe in all my recommendations equally. They are all tools I know are useful for my following. Nevertheless, if the recommendation at the bottom of the page gets the most attention, I'm going to move it up to the top.

Extreme Giving is not about letting go of your integrity. You're not changing what you recommend; you are changing the order.

Imagine you have three favorite movies: Movie A, Movie B, and Movie C. You always recommend them in that order; A, B, C. Most people hate the first movie, half of them like the second movie, and everyone likes the third movie.

Start recommending Movie C first; you'll have more satisfied customers.

They are still your three favorite movies, but now you can better match what you say with what your audience wants to hear. When you recommend something people respond to first, they are more likely to listen to future recommendations.

I vet every product I recommend, because I never want to lower my audience's trust in me.

This is how you can track and improve your business. This is why I out-give everyone I compete with. I always want to give away more free gifts, better free gifts, and more valuable free gifts than everyone else in my industry. I want to be the person you're listening to. My data has shown me Extreme Giving is worth it in the long run.

By looking at my data, I know that providing the most valuable product in a bundle will pay off. Within a year, those customers will spend more money than the original program cost. I can track my customer behavior. This is not an opinion; it's hard data.

My tracking proves that Extreme Giving isn't just a concept in my head. It's a very viable, financially lucrative way of living your life. How cool is that? You get to be a good person, and you get to make more money—double win.

You must look at every metric in your business. What emails are people opening? What links are people clicking? What messages are they responding to?

When working with a consulting client on a book launch, we designed a cover that I knew would rocket his book up the charts. He took one look at the cover and told me a radically different idea for a cover design. I can't share with you the specifics, but I can tell you that many people would have been offended.

The content of the book was superb, but a bad cover would prevent anyone from finding out.

When I explained that his cover idea would prevent people from buying his book, while ours would ensure that he became a bestseller, he agreed to go with our design. We delivered on that promise, and his launch was a massive success.

His plan was to wait until the book became a bestseller and then switch to the design he wanted.

Think about that for a moment. If you're going to take something that's selling like hotcakes and change it, guess what happens to those sales? They're going to plummet.

Fortunately, he never changed the cover, and the book still sells quite well.

Listen to what your customers are saying. If your customers don't like a product, find out why. If people are coming into your store and walking out without buying anything, find out why. Communicate with them. This is where Extreme Giving comes in. You can say, "Before you leave, let me give you a free gift. Thanks for stopping by."

That's what happens when you go to my blog, right?

"Thanks for visiting my blog. I want a chance to bring you back, so I give you a gift so that I can communicate with you."

"Hey, before you leave, let me give you something."

It doesn't have to be something expensive to produce; it just has to be something valuable to the consumer. This can be something as simple as a guide or a list of emergency numbers.

If you're a mechanic, you can provide a list of numbers for someone to call if their car breaks down. Or instructions on how to change a tire in an emergency. Someone breaks down in a place with no cell signal, and that page in their glovebox that they printed off and laminated for about eight cents becomes their lifesaver.

These simple little ideas are how you can stay top-of-mind. You don't have to give a thing; you can give information about something useful. Say, "Hey, you just might need this."

I can't tell you how often people come back because you've given them something valuable. You've given them what they want, and this gives you the ability to track and improve, because now you can reach them again and again.

I don't believe in offering bribes for data. I don't believe in saying, "Hey, if you fill out the survey, we'll give you a coupon." That's how big companies try to get data, and that's why they get broken data.

Someone offered me a twenty-five-dollar Amazon gift card if I would give them some data today. Amazon doesn't deliver where I live, so that's useless to me. You are only going to get data from people who shop at Amazon and think twenty-five dollars is worth an hour of their time. You won't get data from anyone who doesn't fit those two criteria. You won't get any data from your wealthiest customers.

Bribes don't work. Just give value. Say, "I want to help you succeed, even if you don't buy here."

Why do I give away books by other authors to my followers all the time? Shouldn't I worry that my fans will fall in love with another author and leave me?

Good. I would rather you connect with an author you're a ninety-seven percent match with, if we are only a seventy percent match.

I want you to have the best person in front of you. I have no problem with that. I want you to succeed. Remember, I believe in you. It all connects.

I believe in you. Therefore, I want the best coach, trainer, or mentor in front of you—even if it's not me.

Often, stopping things that are not working leads to better results than doubling down on the things that are. When I switched from phone calls to texts, I started going on a lot of dates. And a lot of them ended in disaster.

I studied every date to see what I could have done better. What went right and what went wrong? By looking at the data, I realized that I'm terrible at dinner dates.

I never had a second date with a woman, after a dinner date, in my entire life. It never happened. That's how I know I'm not good at dinner dates. The data told me. If I hadn't been paying attention to the data (which many of us don't), I would still have gone on dinner dates, and I would not have a wife—let alone four kids.

The data is everything. I paid attention to what the kids responded to during the entire time I worked for that charity, and I never brought up God once. Not in a single conversation, because I realized it's a turnoff.

From watching my coworkers, I noticed that people don't like it shoved in their faces. I would be surprised if you can even tell what religion I follow, from this book. You would have to make assumptions about me. Religion was the smallest part of what I was doing. My job was not to give people religion; my job was to give people hope.

God only came up if people asked me. If you ask me about it, I'll tell you about it. If you don't ask me, I will never bring it up. It's my job to lead a life and to communicate with you in a way that gives you hope, not to force my religion upon you. If I lead the right kind of life, that should be attractive and interesting enough.

After seeing my coworker fail, I never repeated her mistake—because I tracked the data, learned from it, and improved.

EXTREME GIVING IN ACTION

Think of Extreme Giving as the yellow brick road that takes you and your business where you want to go. Extreme Giving is how you can outperform the competition, and one key to Extreme Giving is breadth.

Extreme Giving allows you to reach a larger audience.

If you Extreme Give to one hundred people, ninety of them will probably respond positively. But I can't guarantee that it's always going to work on the first person you approach. They might be part of that ten percent that doesn't quite respond.

Giving to one person may feel weird for that person, but when you Extreme Give and give as much value as possible to everyone with whom you interact, that's when you can light up the stars.

Extreme Giving in action is simple.

Let's say that you run a dog training business. When someone visits your website, you can offer them a free guide on how to potty-train their dog in exchange for their email address. After they read that guide, they will immediately receive a second guide about healthy eating for their dog or dealing with a dog that barks too much.

You always want to give an extra piece of value.

You know your market better than I do, so whatever the next questions people have are, give them free guides that answer those questions. That's a simple way to start this process.

You can also send them to three different blog posts that each have a lot of content about something they were interested in. You want to establish a relationship, and the easiest way to do that is by giving.

If you're a dog expert, you can host special events where you invite dog experts from around the world, including dog trainers, dog breeders, and dog show winners. They can give amazing talks about their dog whispering secrets, and all people have to do to get access to that amazing content is just hang out with you.

When people see I am constantly giving away free talks and content on my podcast and blog, they start to feel overwhelmed with kindness. This puts you in a powerful position, because you're the person who gives them access to a magical world of free content. Even though all of those other products in your market are amazing, you're still people's source. You're the connection that gets them inside of that nightclub filled with their dog-training celebrities.

The Extreme Giving mindset is critical.

You might try to monetize as quickly as possible, because this is about building a business. I'm absolutely in favor of you making money, but our first mindset has to be to give and meet people where they are. It's not about charging as much as you can.

There are ways to maximize your revenue by leveraging the breadth of your audience, such as selling more units at a lower price point. But all of that comes from giving as much as we can and looking for opportunities to out-give the competition. We're looking for a chance to show people who visit our websites and stores that we're the best in the market.

PROFIT ALWAYS FOLLOWS GIVING

"Jonathan, if you don't start bringing up God with these kids, they're never going to have that conversation." This was the advice I got from one of my managers. If you don't go for the sale at the first opportunity, you'll never make one.

I had a problem with my regional manager: my team leader was dating him. So, if I had a problem with my team leader, I had to go to her boss, who was also her boyfriend.

On the very first day, I told them I was uncomfortable with the arrangement. My regional manager promised to stay objective and guaranteed that he would never let his personal relationship affect his interactions with me.

Let's skip to the end of the story. He lied.

It's not much of a surprise. Would you want your immediate boss to date their boss?

When you spend all your free time with someone, their opinions are going to affect you far more than someone you only see at work.

When I told my regional manager that I disagreed with his girlfriend's advice to me, he told me to shut up. It was her second year in the program, so she automatically had more wisdom than me—despite the fact that I was four years older than her.

He told me bringing up my age was stupid, and he really didn't appreciate that I mentioned that he was the regional manager based on his age and experience. That day I learned that experience doesn't count unless it's within this organization.

Every time you start a new job, you get to be a freshman in high school again.

That's not how I structure my business. I hire experts because I want to leverage their experience, not throw it away.

Despite my manager's advice, I never went for the sale with the teenagers. I didn't have to.

There is a reason I waited so long to bring up money in this book. It's the easiest part of the process. If you follow everything else in the book, the money will just happen.

If you go where the people are, show them you belong, and give them what they want, they're going to engage with you. If you engage with them by keeping your promises, showing that you believe in them, and keeping them interested, they're going to move into the profit phase. That means they'll pay attention to your recommendations.

You can improve your recommendations by paying attention, which means you'll make a lot of money. Profit always follows giving. I have never sold a product to someone I haven't given something to first.

Throughout the year, instead of listening to my boss and her boss-boyfriend, I paid attention to the data. I focused on engagement rather than sales.

My coworkers all focused on the sale. In our final meeting, when I asked, "How many of you have had a meaningful conversation with a child about hope or religion," none of them could raise their hands.

My coworkers hated me; my success became a critique of their failure.

There's nothing worse than hanging out with someone who used to be like you but improved their life. Every single day they remind you that you could have had the same life if you'd put in the effort. All of your excuses disappear, because there's proof that if you'd taken action, your life would be different. Whether it's losing weight, making more money, or getting better at a sport.

I now lead a large team. In the past year, we've grown from two, to twenty employees. And that growth isn't slowing down.

Despite all that growth, we have zero people in the sales department. Our largest two departments are free content and outreach. The outreach team finds the books we give away every month.

Our company focuses our energy on giving stuff away. That's how I direct my financial resources, because I know that if I give the right things to the right people in the right places, everything else will fall into place. I don't even have to worry about the rest of it.

The numbers are consistent and grow every time I put more energy into giving. A great way to measure me—Jonathan, leader of *Serve No Master*, head of this company, the face, the inventor, the founder—is through what I spend most of my time doing each week. I spend more time creating free blog posts, videos, podcast episodes, interviews, training, and events, than I do creating content that I will sell.

I spend less than twenty percent of my time each week on profit generation. And that usually revolves around talking to other people, finding things to recommend, and then writing emails to tell my audience what I found for them this week.

I don't do the hard sell; I don't need to. I don't want to, because I want a long-term relationship. I would rather you not buy a product if it's not the right fit, even if I would make a bunch of money. I'd rather have you buy something way cheaper six months from now, if it's the right fit for you. Absolutely.

I want to have a relationship with you that will last a few years. I want to be there with you from the beginning, all the way to the end of your journey. I want to see you succeed.

I'm in a lot of markets, and teaching people to build their own business is just one of them. In every single market I enter, the principle has held true that if you give continuously, everything else comes together. When you practice Extreme Giving, people want to hang out with you.

People email me asking for affiliate links to products I've never recommended. Even though they found out about it somewhere else, they want me to get the commission. Why? Because of our engagement, our relationship.

One client purchased an hour-long coaching call from me just to thank me. He wanted to reward me for content that had changed his life. He read one of my dating books, and it led him to an amazing relationship with his girlfriend.

We spent an hour talking. I answered some book questions, and it was totally amazing. When you help people, transform them, and give them value, they come back to you.

We buy products and listen to recommendations from the people we like. If you don't like me, it doesn't matter how good my products are. It doesn't matter how great my training is or if I have the best deal in town—you won't buy from me.

One of the great freedoms of having no boss is that I no longer have to interact with people I don't like.

When I was working at that large company in phone sales, there was a bully. I was in my mid-twenties working for one of the largest companies in the world, and I had someone who would put me into a chokehold while I was on a call with a customer. When I told my manager, she put him onto another shift, and I never saw him again. But I'm still amazed that adults do that.

Every single job I've ever had, I've worked with people that I either did not like, did not respect, or did not feel comfortable around.

When I was working for this charity, for this organization, there was a moment where another volunteer approached me. Everyone could see us, because we were right outside the window. She said something inappropriate to me, and I said, "I feel uncomfortable. I don't want to have a conversation with you in private. I don't want us to ever be in private like this." I felt very, very uncomfortable.

We were outside for less than a minute, and we were visible to every single one of my coworkers. I went back inside, and I said, "If you want to have this conversation, we can have it where other people can hear. I don't feel comfortable."

The next day, my team lead's boyfriend, who was also her boss, called me to have a meeting with him and one of the other leaders of the organization. They said that this girl accused me of saying some mean stuff to her. I said, "Can I explain what happened?" and they said, "You're not allowed to defend yourself." Then something happened that I'll never forget. For the first time in my life, some-one called me a monster and meant it.

Here's the most important part of the story. A year earlier, that exact same girl had had an incident with this same manager who was now standing in front of me. She'd said something inappropriate to him, and he hadn't responded the way she'd wanted. So, she pushed him down a flight of stairs and hurt him.

He listened to someone who'd done the same thing to him and had physically hurt him. He'd had to go to the hospital. And yet, he said to me, "You're not allowed to defend yourself." This was one of those powerful moments in my life. I realized I was working with people who would do whatever it took to get rid of me.

I was having the most meaningful conversa-tions with the children. I had the most powerful relationships and connections, always in a public place. I would never put myself in a situation where something inappropriate could happen. Not in a million years.

That's how I said it. I said, "Her accusations are obviously false. When this happened, we were three feet away. You were looking at me through the window."

He was one of the very witnesses who could prove that the crime hadn't happened. He'd been looking through the window for the entire incident. But that didn't matter. She said I'd called her some mean names, so I was stuck with this poor relationship.

From that point forward, this guy, who'd been harmed by the exact same person, dedicated his life to damaging me in every way he could. He tried to damage me at my part-time job. He even tried to damage my relationship with the children I was working with and seeing transformations in.

He never had a sale. He never had a transformative conversation with a child. He never got children to hope, because he was so busy thinking about himself.

This is a story I've never told before, because I hate it. I hate even the thought that I would do something untoward. This is why I am never in private, where people can't see me. I don't want there to even be the possibility of miscommunication, especially in this environment.

When I'd asked for the right to defend myself, they'd denied it.

They're no longer in that business, because they violated the relationship with their clients by trying to put the sale first. They violated their relationship with me. They had an unethical relationship. Your boss and their boss should not be in a relationship with each other, because it means that you are not safe.

That's what happened to me. At the very beginning of the year, when I'd asked what would happen if I came to him with a problem, he'd promised he would listen to me.

However, when I had a problem, he said, "You're not allowed to defend yourself."

They'd already decided I was guilty before I even walked into the meeting. He trusted someone who had pushed him down a flight of stairs over me, because I was making the most sales. Fortunately, I don't have to work with people like that anymore.

People who break trust with their employees will also break trust with their customers. It's no surprise that business no longer exists.

I have built an empire because I focus on giving.

I had more relationships with, helped, and was there for more of the kids I was paid to help than everyone else in the organization combined. They were so focused on their meetings with each other, their little games, and their gossiping. They focused on the journey, not the destination.

I have never been in that business.

It's the same reason that an employee who doesn't care about generating profit can't fit in with a profit-driven company. The money we make is how we pay everyone's salaries. The only thing that mattered was being there for the kids, not for the other workers.

Besides pushing my boss's boss down a flight of stairs the year before, my accuser had had several complaints lodged against her from the kids we were supposed to be helping. Every time a kid complained about her behavior, the leaders would side with this girl.

If you focus on the profit and bring up the product at the beginning of the conversation, you're going to lose the possibility to connect with that person later. You're going to lose all of your credibility. The Ladder of Trust will collapse.

If you just focus on being the best person you can be and treating people right, things will fall where they're supposed to.

I've never told this story before. It really hurt my feelings. Nevertheless, as with every dark cloud, there is a silver lining. Every time one of my coworkers would badmouth me, one of the kids would defend me.

The same children who were growing up in a place of no hope. The same children who had traumatic and painful relationships with adults and their parents. The same children who adults treated with indifference, did not believe in, or never gave hope and light. The same children who believed that they had a life that was going nowhere—they were the ones who defended me.

That is the only measurement that matters.

In that business, the true measurement of sales was if I could form relationships where I could help people and give people hope. The fact that they stood up for me when they didn't have to warms my heart. It makes it all worth it.

In the same way, it's worth it when a customer emails me saying they went through one of my programs and left the job they hated. They don't have to listen to anyone else. They don't have to work with someone who makes them feel bad.

They no longer live in fear of a trial without evidence.

I could have proven I was innocent in less than three minutes of conversation, but they silenced me. I don't want anyone to have that much power over you. That is why I'm teaching you the most powerful business model in the world.

Every time I want to make more money, I just do more giving. I hire more outreach people whose entire job is to give. I make as much free content and training as I can that works. You can go through all my free training, never have to buy a course from me, and build a massively successful business. You can make a lot of money, all without buying anything from me.

I have no problem with you doing that; I encourage you to do it. I love those success stories. If you can't afford to buy one of my courses, don't buy it. Stick to the free stuff. You will make enough money so that one day you can afford the good stuff. That's the beauty of Extreme Giving: when you give, give, give, your customers will be there for you when you need them the most.

CHAPTER SIX

I wasn't the only one who struggled within that charity organization. I had a friend in the organization who was unbelievable. He came from a dire upbringing, a hard place, so he played the types of music kids like that enjoyed. It's the genre of music called "garage", that we don't even have in America. He was very good at it. He always had the coolest haircuts, and he knew how to breakdance.

After his second year in the organization, they told him he wasn't the type of person they wanted in there. He was basically the 'me' of another location. He had had so many meaningful conversations. He was the type of person that I wished I could be.

He got it.

My parents never hurt me, so I can only have empathy if that happened to you. I can care about you. I can do everything I can, but I'll never know what it's like to have an adult hurt me. A few years ago, my wife and I moved, to protect one of our children from another adult. I know what it's like to be scared for your child's safety. I don't know what it's like to be the victim, but I know what it's like to be on the parental side.

I have many friends who have been victims, including this amazing charity worker. He'd been through some tough stuff. It's not my place to share the specifics, but he connected with these people because he knows what it's like to be scared. He knows what it's like when people don't believe in you. He was crushing it in the sales department.

The same people that didn't believe in me didn't believe in him either. They called me a monster, and they said he was the kind of person that they didn't want in their organization. Amazing. When your entire organization is built around transforming teenage lives, the person you should fire is not the person who is the most transformative.

When you try to go it alone, you will be limited. You will struggle, and you will fight. You absolutely can build a business as an army of one, but it is so much harder than when you bring Extreme Giving into your alliances.

This amazing friend gave me so much. He gave me training, kindness, attention, support and he helped me become a better musician. He taught me how to breakdance (even though my body is not designed for breakdancing) and he gave me the strength to be transformative in my career.

BUILDING ALONE IS HARD

There were many times during that year I felt alone. While I had a lot of success and had amazing relationships with my "customers" (these children from tough backgrounds), I didn't have friends within my organization. I didn't have friends, because my coworkers focused on becoming friends with each other, to the detriment of the children we were being paid to help.

I can't do that. I cannot abide by that. I cannot sell a product that does not work, and I cannot treat my customers, whoever they are, with less than one hundred percent. It just isn't in my DNA. I discovered that as I began to form relationships with some of the older kids, they would help me with the younger kids. That's a powerful place to be.

When I started out as an author, I saw every other author with a book similar to mine as competition. They're trying to steal my customers. You have a podcast. I have a podcast. Why would I have you as a guest on my show if all you're going to do is steal my customers?

I held the belief that I had to fight on my own, make this work on my own, and my competition was standing between my customers and me.

This is the wrong approach. I was friends with some other people in the organization who were transformative. The organization eventually threw them all away. They kicked out all of my friends. Every single one of my friends was told, "You're no longer welcome in this organization."

I looked it up today and discovered the entire organization no longer exists. I haven't thought about the organization or this story for almost twenty years. I've never told these stories to anyone, not even my wife. Unless she reads this book, she'll never hear them.

When you try to go it alone, you fight for every customer.

When I read a book by a new author, it doesn't make me stop liking other books I've read in the past. Every time I finish reading a book on my e-reader, it recommends a new book for me to read next. Because of the power of recommendation, I go check it out, and now I like another author.

When I had the Extreme Giving revelation, I stopped worrying about losing customers. When I let go of that, my business grew sevenfold in one year and tenfold the next year. Because I let go of the fear of competition, my company grew seventy times over. I stopped focusing on profit and started focusing on the customer.

If I'm the wrong person for you to follow, I will introduce you to the right person. Yes, I'll make less money, but if your life is better, haven't I done a thing of goodness?

It all circles back to trying to put more good into the world than bad. The more you focus on the good, the more the profit follows. This is how I approach the growth of my business. Instead of trying to build it alone, I create cooperative events all the time. I run at least two cooperative events a month. We're accelerating that to three, and soon it'll be up to four.

Every single week you hang out with me, you get more free stuff. I've worked with other authors who I've introduced to more new readers in a weekend than they've gathered in the previous two years. It puts a smile on my face when I hear that.

Let's say you run a small business in your town and the same hundred customers come to you every week. You can approach nine other businesses with the same sized customer bases. You invite them to join you in throwing a party where you'll introduce your products to each other's customers.

The grocery store, the hardware store, the clothing store, the bookstore, and six other stores all get together to throw an event. You let everyone know, "Hey, we're all friends with each other, we have a circle together, and here's what we offer. We're all throwing a block party and giving away a bunch of cool free stuff."

Each of you'd had the same sized business, with one hundred customers. By joining forces, your event now has a thousand people. Nine hundred of those people have never set foot in your store or set eyes on your sign. Now, they get to meet you face-to-face and talk to you. Now, you can connect with them, show that you belong, and give them what they want. Now, you have a chance to form a relationship.

Even if ninety percent of the new people hate what you are doing, you will still double your audience size. Most of the time, a majority of people hating you is a failure. But with the power of cooperation, you can fail your way to doubling your business.

I love working with other authors, and I'm not afraid of other authors, speakers, or competitors. I want us to grow together. A rising tide raises all ships. That's in many of the outreach emails I send out. I'm always looking for ways to work with other people. I love cooperative ventures, and I love working together.

I love succeeding together. It's very important to me, because I know that going alone is hard. I've had to go alone before. If I hadn't had a group of people that were in alignment with me—my support group—I wouldn't have been able to go the distance. I wouldn't have been able to have as much success as I did during my year of charity.

GIVE FIRST

EXTREME COLLABORATION

I love holding collaborative events and organizing conferences, because I don't have to establish all the value. The more partners I work with on a project, the better. The easiest way to bring all of my partners together is by hosting an Extreme Alliance event.

An Extreme Alliance event is just like a summer festival.

Let's say I organize an event with ten bands. Your favorite band is playing with nine bands you've never heard of. You show up for one band, but the other nine have a chance to impress you. They get the value of exposure to you, your favorite band gets exposure to the fans of nine other bands, and the audience gets to see their favorite band and experience some new bands.

Organizing a collaborative event that gives the customer and participants value ensures everyone wins.

Whatever your market, look at your "competition" and ask yourself if there is a way that you could work with them. Is there a way that you can gain access to their audience that is a win for them?

The beauty of group events is that the total is greater than the sum of its parts. Even if each band at our festival only brings one hundred pre-existing fans, the power of the Extreme Alliance allows them to play in front of an audience of one thousand people. They may not convert the entire crowd into new fans, but they will surely capture a few of them.

You can't grow with no audience; as the event organizer, you can build an audience the fastest. People will come to your festival, even if they don't know most of the bands. You can build an entire brand around Extreme Alliances.

For each event, you invite ten new bands, and your following doubles in size. There are so many festivals that people buy tickets for before the bands are even announced. That could be you.

INVESTED IN YOUR SUCCESS

When people feel like they played a role in the creation of a product, they become more invested in its success. These powerful connections make them far more likely to talk about it.

If I included a quote from you in this book, would that get you excited? Instead of saying that Jonathan just released a new book, you could brag that your quote is in it. Your recommendation changes from "I think this is pretty cool" to "I'm a part of it."

Instead of mentioning the book to a few people, you'll mention it to everyone you know, because you are a part of the success. As my book moves up the bestseller charts, so does your sense of self and good feeling, because you are part of something.

That little piece of ownership will change how you feel and how you promote a product. And that's the feeling you want to give to every person with whom you collaborate.

We've already talked about the power of reciprocity to get customers to buy our product. Now, we're going to use that same effect to get other businesses on our team. When I do a favor for you, you'll feel inspired to do a favor for me, and that inspiration is compounded when we add the Ownership Effect.

This effect supersedes the traditional affiliate marketing paradigm. You'll generate far more sales by motivating affiliates, partners, and collaborators using the ownership effect than you will by offering them more money.

When we organize collaborative events, your affiliates transform into partners. They are promoting something they've played an active role in building. That's a lot more exciting than simply recommending another product to their audience.

When I organize a book giveaway, each author tells their audience they are part of something great.

They are playing at a festival. This is far more effective than asking them to tell their audience about a festival where they aren't playing. You can offer a cut of the tickets they sell, but you'd be hard-pressed to find a single band to promote a concert where they aren't playing. So don't do it in business.

Every time you are thinking about collaborating with someone, ask yourself how you can give them a sense of ownership in the event.

GIVE TO THEIR FOLLOWERS

During my year of charity, many of my coworkers were unavailable to our customers—these children—outside of office hours. If we weren't officially at the cafe, if it wasn't officially open, or if we weren't on a specific job, then it was their "free time." This means they never had a conversation with a child who did not come into the cafe. If you hung out across the street or stayed outside, they never spoke to you.

If you tried to forge a relationship with a kid who was coming to the cafe and all their friends weren't, you created a bigger trust gap between them and their friends. Their friends would say, "Well, that adult never talks to us. I don't know why you trust them." That's how kids think.

I talked to those kids all the time. I would meet with them when I was out in the world. They would see me at parties and raves all the time. I was never enhanced or even drinking, because I was always on duty. They would have meaningful conversations with me because of this. The friends who never came into the cafe would say, "Jonathan's cool with us. It's cool that you're friends with him."

Someone could ask me about God, life, hope, becoming an adult, or finding a job. They could ask me about their messed-up relationship, the things they're scared about, or dealing with enhancements. They could ask me anything - without feeling like they were betraying their friends.

Their friends would say things like, "He's an adult, but he's not that bad." It isn't as good as cool, but "not that bad"? I'll take it. I'll take it from teenagers, because some of this stuff teenagers can say is really mean. So, I will take a "not that bad" with a smile on my face.

Don't ask your competitors to bring all their customers to your store because you're having a party and will pay them a percentage of everything their followers buy. It will just turn them off.

When people reach out to me with promises of how much money I'll make, it doesn't get my attention. I run a business, so I obviously care about money. I'd be lying if I said I didn't. But that's not the messaging I respond to.

Before I even entertain recommending your product to my audience, I need to know that it works. I need to know that it will benefit the people I have spent so much time building trust with.

When I ask if the program works, sometimes people say things like, "What difference does it make? You will make a bunch of money." That's a big red flag for me. I don't do business with people like that.

I care about my customers; I care about my clients. I'm passionate about them, and I believe in them. I form relationships with them, and I have to be honest with them. That means I can only recommend things I believe in.

If you recommend things you don't believe in, you might make that big payday, but those people will never talk to you again. You'll spend your life constantly trying to replace all the customers you've lost because of broken promises. That's too hard.

When I reach out, I first talk about giving them value, and then I immediately talk about giving value to their audience.

"I want to give your audience something amazing. I want to share your book with my audience, and I would love to share sixteen other free books with your audience. I would love to give a lot of valuable free stuff to your audience."

That's how you connect with amazing people. People who care about their customers only want to work with other people who care about their customers.

If you focus on Extreme Giving in every area of your business, toward your own customers, and toward other people's customers, they'll feel comfortable introducing you to their followers. Remember, the introduction is so powerful. If I introduce someone to you and you break their trust, that will damage their relationship with me.

Last year, a friend I really trusted introduced me to someone for a project. That person betrayed my trust and turned out to be quite unethical. My friend had brought me into a business project with someone who tried to steal money from another friend of mine, and followed this by not responding to my messages.

I am still trying to repair all of those other relationships that this person damaged by working on a project with me for six months. I told my friend, who'd made the introduction, that he'd damaged our relationship as well. He didn't know how the project would end, but I haven't spoken to him in months.

Let's stop talking about me and get back to talking about you.

If you are throwing an amazing event where the entire focus is on your business, nobody will want to collaborate with you. If your partners walk in with one hundred customers and walk out with ninety, they will never speak to you again. Nobody wants to decrease their customer base.

Show partners you care about them, their friends, and their customers. Demonstrate generosity through words and actions. If your customers, partners, and employees speak highly of you and your company, new partners are going to give you a shot.

You must focus on the heart of giving. You're going to make a lot of mistakes along the way if you pretend to be an Extreme Giver. If you try to replicate the process without believing in the philosophy, you'll slip up. You'll make tiny mistakes that cause the entire house of cards to come crashing down.

You'll approach potential partners and collaborators, offering them bags of money, and forget to mention their audience. You'll slip up, because it's hard to fake Extreme Giving.

It's absolutely, positively necessary for you to give in every direction. Give to your customers, the people you want to form Extreme Alliances with, and their customers. When you do this, everything will come into place, and your business will grow. Amazing partners will bring you traffic, engagement, and profits.

EXTREME ALLIANCES IN ACTION

ORGANIZED GIVEAWAYS

What better way to kick off your new alliance than by merging all your Extreme Gifts into a massive free-gift bonanza? When Extreme Givers work together, everybody benefits.

I love to organize book giveaways.

If an author joins one of my events and makes their book free for my audience, they're going to get new followers. Not only does this system benefit my audience, but it also benefits my partners.

When I stopped focusing on selling copies of *Serve No Master* and started giving them away, my business exploded, and my audience expanded.

This simple mindset shift allowed me to partner with authors that I'd been competing with for years. We were fighting for our positions in the same categories. We were all investing more and more resources to capture the exact same readers.

My ad costs skyrocketed from five cents per visitor for my book listing to over a dollar. My marketing costs went up twentyfold, and I realized it wasn't sustainable. I needed a new method.

I reached out to those same authors that I'd been bidding against and offered to share their book with my audience if they shared my book with theirs. With this system, we'd all win without spending more money on advertising.

Promotional events are a cooperative venture, so this is an easy way to find a circle of other authors with whom you can work.

You don't need a large audience to organize your first giveaway. If twenty authors each send twenty visitors, you have four hundred visitors who will at least see the cover of your book.

You always get more than you give in these promotions. They are like a magic car from a Dr. Seuss book - powered by a generator that makes more power than it uses. Giving events are the easiest ways to gain followers and create alliances.

PRODUCT BUNDLES

A product bundle is just a giveaway that's paid for.

I take part in these often, because I love getting my name in front of new people. These events have an additional layer of complexity, because they now involve money. Someone has to handle all the cash and make sure everyone gets paid. The simplest version of this is selling twenty books for twenty dollars.

Now it's exactly like our book giveaway.

When organizing these events, make sure that your tracking system is bulletproof. The last thing you want is a mistake when money is involved. When in doubt, over-deliver to your partners.

When hosting a bundle promotion, you want everyone to include products of comparable value. I like to give away the most expensive product when I participate in an event, but if I were to include a two-thousand-dollar course while everyone else was giving away a ten-dollar book, it would destroy the balance of the event.

Some participants in these events just want to give away the minimum amount required to participate. They give away products they've never sold before and coupons.

They make their "product" the previous night and give it a random value.

Make sure your participants have the same giving heart as you do. The ones who give away the worst products will get the worst return on their investment. The ones who give away products with actual value will capture the most new followers. Teach your new allies that their generosity will be rewarded.

Whether I am organizing an event or merely participating, I want to develop a reputation as someone who gives you more than you expected - in every phase of our relationship.

If you get something from me for free, I want it to feel better than when someone else gives you something for free. If you pay ten dollars, I want to give you something worth one hundred. If you pay one thousand dollars, I want to give you something worth ten thousand. Whatever you put in, I want to give you more value than that.

When organizing your event, the goal is to give each customer the maximum value for every dollar they spend. The better the products in your bundle, the happier your customers will be. With amazing products, your allies will make more sales. They will make more money.

That's the perfect event: satisfied customers and allies.

VIRTUAL EVENTS

A virtual event is simply a digital version of a live event. Just like our collaboration with ten bands, everyone records a talk, the organizer compiles all the videos, and the audience can watch at their leisure. It's a great way to integrate your partners' products, services, and expertise into your events.

Organizing these types of events is more challenging than giveaways, so I would recommend participating as a speaker first. All you have to do is give an interview, and at the end, you can advertise your Extreme Gift. When the event is live, you can email your existing audience to tell them you are being interviewed during the event.

When I organize an event, I always consider how I can make it better than other organizers for my potential speakers. I want my speakers to have an amazing experience, so they recommend my events to all of their friends.

When you're ready to organize your own event, look at how the events you took part in recruited you. Copy what they did right and improve what they did wrong. Don't be afraid to learn from their mistakes.

As long as you follow this process, you'll become the top event organizer in your niche.

If you already have the mindset of giving more value or providing a better experience to your participants, live events will be easier to do. When you share your best material during talks and then give away something of massive value for free, people will want to follow you and hear your message, and you will outperform everyone else.

I've been to events where I experienced more growth than people with much bigger followings, because I gave the most value.

COLLABORATIVE CONTENT

I love letting other people create content for me.

You can build collaborative courses with guest interviews and instructors. When they create even one component of the product, it will give them a sense of ownership. The more you integrate your ally's efforts into the product or the launch, the greater that sense of ownership and the greater the effect of collaboration will become. My allies create the content, and all I have to do is compile everything and organize it into an easily consumable package for my audience.

I don't need to turn all my collaborators into coaches when I launch my coaching program. They don't have to meet with my audience every week, and they don't have to become invested in the coaching process.

Instead, I interview ten people with whom I want to collaborate and get each of them to generate a chapter for an e-book that I will give away for free at the start of my coaching funnel. They can share the book with their audience without even needing to mention my coaching product.

When they share something with their name on it, sales will increase. If you put their name and picture on the book cover, you'll get even better results. Their audience already knows, likes, and trusts them. I'm simply leveraging that likability and trust in a way that's positive for everyone involved.

Results will always be larger when the person promoting us has their name on what they're promoting. That's one reason you can typically get such high conversion rates with Extreme Collaboration. Therefore, event marketing with collaboration outperforms paid traffic. You have a level of endorsement that money just can't buy.

They don't have to be a part of the primary product and coach all of my followers. Instead, they can promote a small book to their audience, and they'll likely promote it with more energy than any other product they have recommended in the past. Their messaging changes from recommending a training course by some guy they know to recommending a book they're part of.

It's a slight change, but their audience will respond to it much more strongly.

Even better, you will receive the benefit of transferring authority.

It's easier for someone to promote a book they helped create than it is to send their audience to a book to which they have no connection.

They're not just promoting a free book; they're promoting their effort that went into creating that free book. They're selling their expertise, and that's much more likely to connect to their audience.

It's far easier for someone to give a compelling reason their audience should download this free book than for anything they promote that they're not a part of.

Which are you more likely to get excited by: a book where I wrote a chapter, or a book by a friend of mine? No matter how much I talk up my friend, they are an unknown variable. You might not like them. In the book with my chapter, you know you'll have at least one chapter that you want to read.

The added benefit of this system is that you get your collaborators to do all the work, and it's a super win for you. Someone else makes and promotes the product, and all you have to do is compile everything and organize it. You put their names on the landing page or the cover of the book, and you've fulfilled your collaboration component.

You've killed two birds with one stone. You have a great product that leveraged other people's creative content, along with passionate partners who'll share the book with as many people as they can. And all you have to do is sit back and wait for the customers to come flooding in.

There are multiple ways that you can benefit and approach things collaboratively as a business owner and a product creator, and the power of teamwork will absolutely magnify every aspect of your Extreme Giving.

THE EXTREME MINDSET

Your mindset for every event in which you participate should be to give more value to both a potential partner and their audience than you take from them.

You might consider just giving your book to their audience, but that's not enough. Think of a creative message that will take you beyond that. Ask them if there's anything you can do to support them and help them grow. Offer help that seems to benefit them more than it benefits you.

A car salesman I worked with once told me, "A good deal is one where both people walk away happy."

That's what you want to create: a wonderful experience in which, months later, nobody regrets taking part. You want them to want to come back.

People participating in my events always tell me they've never had a bigger success than working on my event. Because they've never had a better experience, they hope I will host more events and invite them to the next one, and they'll be more than happy to join.

It's easy to get people to participate when you over-give. Your mindset should always be to give more than you get. When you do, it's easy to run an Extreme Giving business.

THE END OF THE ROAD

Every movie has an ending, every cowboy has a last ride, and every sun sets. Every book has to have a final chapter, and we're now there.

At the beginning of this book, I told you about a young boy whose parents were living on welfare and told him not to waste his time going to school or trying, because he was always just going to be on welfare, just like them. They said that he would live in a government house with them until one day the government would give him his own house. That his kids would live on welfare, and those kids would go to public school on welfare, live in government housing, and never be productive members of society.

I spent a lot of time with him. I went to his DJ gigs, and I ran into him at nightclubs when none of the other people from my organization were there. When I ran into him, sometimes he was enhanced. You're not supposed to do that when you're a teenager, but it happens.

Never once did I judge him. Never once did I belittle him. Never once did I blow up his spot when I ran into his friends I'd never seen at the cafe. I believed in him. Now, he's a successful musician running his own events and making his way in the world. Nothing else matters.

There was another child I worked with who no one else believed in. They told her she could never do anything. They told her she could never be a musician, and she'd never be successful because of her limitations. I can't go into any more detail, because now she's a TV star. How cool is that?

I believed in her; we believed in her. Enough that she started to believe in herself and went for an audition that she would never have considered before that. Very cool. I might be an adult, but maybe I am "not that bad."

If you can embed this philosophy into your own life, you can become the person to whom children without hope will talk. You can become the person to whom people who feel lonely listen. You can become the person whose business they want to come into — a person from whom they want to buy and with whom they want to connect, because they like and trust you.

People will respect you because they feel a connection with you. You're the first person to treat them as more than a commodity or a statistic or a number. This is a powerful and transformative philosophy, and it can make you very wealthy.

I have an unbelievable lifestyle. I surf every day. It's always sunny on my little island. My children are healthy, and my wife is healthy. We have a house bigger than I thought I would ever live in. We have three dogs, which is more dogs than I ever thought I would have. I only bought one of them. I don't even know how the other two got here, but we have an amazing life.

My hope was to give my children a better life than I'd had. My dad set the bar very high. My dad never hurt me. My dad provided for me. My dad believed in me.

My one regret was that my dad wasn't around very much.

Before you think he dropped the ball, my dad never missed an event. He was at every single sports

game of my entire life. Every type of competition—
he was there. He was there when I saved the soccer
game and the crowd went wild. He was there when
I cursed out my coach.

But he worked brutally long hours.

He came home from work long after I came
home from school, and he worked on Saturdays.
He wanted to give us a better life than he'd had
as a child, and he succeeded at that. So, my one
regret was that my dad didn't work from home, and
I get to do that. My dad set the bar high, but the
one thing I wanted to do was to always be there
for my kids.

You guys don't know this, because you can't see
me writing this, but my oldest son was standing on
the second-floor balcony making rude hand gestures
at me while I was dictating the last chapter. He was
smiling, because he's just joking around. He likes to
be a bad boy.

He craves attention, even if it's negative attention. I will not tell you whether or not I made a
naughty gesture back at him. I don't want to get in
trouble with my wife when she reads this book, but
I'm always near my children, because of my heart
of generosity.

My business started from a place that was tough.
We had some tough times and some struggles.
Now it's bullet-proof, recession-proof, and depres-
sion-proof. It can adapt to different storms. I have a
business model that can last a long time, one that my

children will inherit and continue to grow. That's a place where I want you to be.

If you can take the lesson of this book, you can live a life of greatness. If you only remember two words—Extreme Giving. Or, if you just remember *Give to Get*, the title of the book, that's just as good.

I encourage you to hang out on my website, check out my social media channels, podcasts, and videos. I'll just keep giving you free stuff until you fall in love with me. You might've read this book and be part of the ten percent of people that go, "Jonathan is all talk. I don't believe it. No way he gives that much." Challenge accepted.

I will give until it hurts. If it takes a thousand years, then it takes a thousand years. You will see that I live this philosophy, and then you can live it too. You can grow a business that you're proud of and make the world just a little bit better while you do it.

ONE LAST CHANCE

I want to thank you for taking the time to read *Give to Get*. I've spent ten years building a business on the foundation of Extreme Giving, and I am so excited to transform your life. I hope you can take what you've learned and use it to build an amazing business by focusing on giving rather than selling.

This is the easiest and fastest way to grow a business, and it's allowed me to endure multiple market shocks.

This book is the foundation for an amazing business model... but it's just the beginning. In the second book, you'll get step-by-step instructions on how to implement Extreme Giving. The book you hold in your hands is the big picture and the vision for creating an amazing business. When you're ready to take that business to the next level, you're going to LOVE *Give to Get Part 2*: *Advanced Tactics*. And it is yours. Absolutely free. When you click this link:

ServeNoMaster.com/Give

FOUND A TYPO?

While every effort goes into ensuring that this book is flawless, it is inevitable that a mistake or two will have slipped through the cracks.

If you find an error of any kind in this book, please let me know by visiting:

ServeNoMaster.com/Typos

I appreciate you taking the time to notify me of any mistakes you found in this book. This ensures that future readers never have to experience that awful typo.

You are making the world a better place.

ABOUT THE AUTHOR

For ten years, Jonathan was just like many other Americans who were a part of the education merry-go-round. In 2009, he peaked in his profession.

With a fresh Master's degree in hand, a published dissertation, and experience teaching at a university in London, he accepted a position at one of the top twenty universities in America.

Years of planning and strategy came together to land his "dream job." When his first paycheck arrived, he began to realize that his dream was an illusion. Locked into a much lower salary than he imagined for his thirties, the future began to look very bleak indeed.

Then a miracle happened - an ex-girlfriend called his boss and actually got him fired. It was the worst day of his life, but also the best. Jonathan would never have had the confidence to start his own business full time without that kick in the pants.

Within six months, he was making more money than at his "dream job," and less than two years later, he was making more than the lady who fired him.

So many people these days are learning that having a job is not a form of security.

You can lose your job at any moment for thousands of reasons you have no control over. Every day, more super-qualified people are kicked back into the job pool, and they start to flounder.

Everything Jonathan does with *Serve No Master* is to prepare you for that day, even if it hasn't already come. You don't have to quit your job, but opening up new online revenue streams will help protect you.

In a digital world packed with "experts," few people have the experience to tell you how things work, why they work, and what's actually working in the online business world right now.

Altogether, his experience makes him one of the most captivating and accomplished people in the lifestyle design world. He has dedicated his life to sharing the best of what he knows, with total transparency, as part of his mission to free regular people from the 9-5 and live on their own terms.

Learn from his successes and failures... and Serve No Master.

Find out more about Jonathan at ServeNoMaster.com

BOOKS BY JONATHAN GREEN

Non-Fiction

Serve No Master Series
Fire Your Boss
Serve No Master
Breaking Orbit
20K a Day
Control Your Fate
Breakthrough
Give to Get

Authorship Series
Write a Book in Two Hours
Essential Tools for Writers
The Six-Figure Writer
Get Paid More to Write
The Successful Self-Publisher
Book Marketing for Authors
Making a Living as an Author
The Business of Writing Books
Turning Your Job into a Writing Career
Co-Writing a Book
Seven Secrets to Writing a Bestseller

Blogging for Authors
The Writing Habit
Email Marketing for Authors
The Bestseller Habit
Dictation Machine
Book Cover Mastery
How to Write a Successful Book Series

Habit of Success Series
PROCRASTINATION
Influence and Persuasion
Overcome Depression
Stop Worrying and Anxiety
Love Yourself
Conquer Stress
Law of Attraction
Mindfulness (coming soon)
Meditation (coming soon)
I'm Not Shy
Coloring Depression Away with Adult Coloring Books
Don't be Quiet (coming soon)
How to Make Anyone Like You

Develop Good Habits with S.J. Scott
How to Quit Your Smoking Habit
Weight Loss Mastery

Seven Secrets
Seven Networking Secrets for Jobseekers
Seven Secrets to Getting Hired for Jobseekers

Biographies

The Fate of my Father

Complex Adult Coloring Books

The Dinosaur Adult Coloring Book
The Dog Adult Coloring Book
The Celtic Adult Coloring Book
The Outer Space Adult Coloring Book
The 2nd Celtic Adult Coloring Book

Irreverent Coloring Books

Dragons Are Bastards

Fiction

Gunpowder and Magic

The Outlier (As Drake Blackstone)

ONE LAST THING

This is a book about the power of giving, and here is your first chance to see Extreme Giving in action. You can leave a five-star review in less than five seconds. You can give without costing you anything. The more you give, the more people can get the value of this book.

Reviews are the lifeblood of any book on Amazon, especially for an independent author. If you click five stars on your Kindle device or visit the special link below at your convenience, you will ensure that I can continue to produce more books. A quick rating or review helps me to support my family, and I deeply appreciate it.

Without stars and reviews, you would never have found this book. Please take just thirty seconds of your time to support an independent author by leaving a rating.

Thank you so much! To leave a review, go to:

ServeNoMaster.com/GiveToGet

Sincerely,
Jonathan Green
ServeNoMaster.com

www.ingramcontent.com/pod-product-compliance
Lightning Source LLC
Chambersburg PA
CBHW070704190326
41458CB00004B/841